# How to Build, Protect and Maintain Your 401(k) Plan

## Strategies & Tactics

BY DALE ROGERS
& CRAIG ROGERS

MARKETPLACE BOOKS
Columbia, MD

# T RA

# SEC

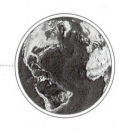

# Titles in the FP Books Trade Secrets Series

**The Life Insurance Handbook**
*By Louis S. Shuntich, J.D., LL.M*

**How to Build, Protect and Maintain Your 401(k) Plan**
*Strategies & Tactics*
*By Dale Rogers & Craig Rogers*

**How to Write an Investment Policy Statement**
*By Jack Gardner*

**Asset Allocation Essentials**
*Simple Steps to Winning Portfolios*
*By Michael C. Thomsett*

**The Long-Term Care Planning Guide**
*Practical Steps for Making Difficult Decisions*
*By Don Korn*

**Understanding ERISA**
*A Compact Guide to the Landmark Act*
*By Ken Ziesenheim*

*Combine knowledge with self discipline and you become unstoppable. This book is intended to give every investor and advisor the knowledge needed to build a safe and secure retirement plan. The discipline is up to you. But—by following the principles outlined in this book, your journey on this path should be easier and, ultimately, more successful.*

— Dale Rogers

This book, along with other books, is available at discounts that make it realistic to provide it as a gift to your customers, clients, and staff. For more information on these long lasting, cost effective premiums, please call us at (800) 272-2855 or you may email us at sales@traderslibrary.com.

ISBN 13 978-1-59280-097-1
ISBN 1-59280-097-1

**Printed in the United States of America.**

1 2 3 4 5 6 7 8 9 0

# Contents

**Introduction**. . . . . . . . . . . . . . . . . . . . . . . . . . . . . . . . . . . . . . . . . . . . 13
Before We Get Started . . . .. . . . . . . . . . . . . . . . . . . . . . . . . . . . . 13
Nine Building Blocks: How to Build, Protect and Maintain
Your 401(k) Plan. . . . . . . . . . . . . . . . . . . . . . . . . . . . . . . . . . . . 15
Acknowledgement . . . . . . . . . . . . . . . . . . . . . . . . . . . . . . . . . . . . 18

**Chapter 1**
LEARN WHAT'S IN YOUR SUMMARY PLAN
DESCRIPTION (SPD). . . . . . . . . . . . . . . . . . . . . . . . . . . . . . . . 19
Eligibility (Who Can Invest?) . . . . . . . . . . . . . . . . . . . . . . . . . . . . 20
Vesting. . . . . . . . . . . . . . . . . . . . . . . . . . . . . . . . . . . . . . . . . . . 21
What Happens in the Event of Your Death?. . . . . . . . . . . . . . . . . . 22
How Are the Funds Paid to Your Beneficiary? . . . . . . . . . . . . . . . . 24
When & Where to Get Help . . . . . . . . . . . . . . . . . . . . . . . . . . . . . 24
Summary . . . . . . . . . . . . . . . . . . . . . . . . . . . . . . . . . . . . . . . . . . 25

**Chapter 2**
LEARN HOW TO PUT MONEY INTO YOUR PLAN . . . . . . . . . .27
How Your Contributions Get Invested . . . . . . . . . . . . . . . . . . . . . . 28
Taking Advantage of Pre-Tax Dollars . . . . . . . . . . . . . . . . . . . . . . 29
Getting Started . . . . . . . . . . . . . . . . . . . . . . . . . . . . . . . . . . . . . . 31
Exponential Growth Through Compounding . . . . . . . . . . . . . . . . . 32
Summary. . . . . . . . . . . . . . . . . . . . . . . . . . . . . . . . . . . . . . . . . . . 34

**Chapter 3**
LEARN HOW EMPLOYER MATCHING FUNDS CAN
ADD MONEY TO YOUR PLAN . . . . . . . . . . . . . . . . . . . .35
Read Your Plan's Fine Print . . . . . . . . . . . . . . . . . . . . . . . . . . . . . . 36
Matching in Company Stock . . . . . . . . . . . . . . . . . . . . . . . . . . . . . 37

Company Stock and Your Job. . . . . . . . . . . . . . . . . . . . . . . . . . . . . . . . 39
Correct Through Diversification . . . . . . . . . . . . . . . . . . . . . . . . . . . . . 39
Summary . . . . . . . . . . . . . . . . . . . . . . . . . . . . . . . . . . . . . . . . . . . . . . . 41

**Chapter 4**

LEARN HOW MUCH RISK YOU SHOULD TAKE . . . . . . . . . . . .43
Everybody Is a Long-Term Investor—Until They Get Their
    Quarterly Statement . . . . . . . . . . . . . . . . . . . . . . . . . . . . . . . . . . . 43
Managing Risk . . . . . . . . . . . . . . . . . . . . . . . . . . . . . . . . . . . . . . . . . 44
What Is Your Tolerance for Risk? . . . . . . . . . . . . . . . . . . . . . . . . . . . 46
Summary . . . . . . . . . . . . . . . . . . . . . . . . . . . . . . . . . . . . . . . . . . . . . . . 48

**Chapter 5**

LEARN ABOUT THE VARIOUS ASSET CLASSES. . . . . . . . . . . . .49
What Are Asset Classes? . . . . . . . . . . . . . . . . . . . . . . . . . . . . . . . . . . 49
Cash. . . . . . . . . . . . . . . . . . . . . . . . . . . . . . . . . . . . . . . . . . . . . . . . . . 49
Bonds . . . . . . . . . . . . . . . . . . . . . . . . . . . . . . . . . . . . . . . . . . . . . . . . 50
Equities . . . . . . . . . . . . . . . . . . . . . . . . . . . . . . . . . . . . . . . . . . . . . . . 50
Large-Cap Growth. . . . . . . . . . . . . . . . . . . . . . . . . . . . . . . . . . . . . . . 51
S & P 500 . . . . . . . . . . . . . . . . . . . . . . . . . . . . . . . . . . . . . . . . . . . . . 51
Large-Cap Value . . . . . . . . . . . . . . . . . . . . . . . . . . . . . . . . . . . . . . . . 52
U.S. Small-Cap Growth . . . . . . . . . . . . . . . . . . . . . . . . . . . . . . . . . . 52
U.S. Small-Cap Value . . . . . . . . . . . . . . . . . . . . . . . . . . . . . . . . . . . . 52
International . . . . . . . . . . . . . . . . . . . . . . . . . . . . . . . . . . . . . . . . . . . . 52
Rate of Returns by Asset Class . . . . . . . . . . . . . . . . . . . . . . . . . . . . . 53
Summary . . . . . . . . . . . . . . . . . . . . . . . . . . . . . . . . . . . . . . . . . . . . . . . 59

**Chapter 6**

LEARN THE SIX PRINCIPLES OF SUCCESSFUL INVESTING .61
Investing Is a Marathon, Not a Sprint! . . . . . . . . . . . . . . . . . . . . . . . . 61
Principle One—Dollar Cost Averaging. . . . . . . . . . . . . . . . . . . . . . . . 62
Principle Two—Diversification . . . . . . . . . . . . . . . . . . . . . . . . . . . . . 65
Principle Three—Asset Allocation. . . . . . . . . . . . . . . . . . . . . . . . . . . 66
Principle Four—Asset-Class Investing . . . . . . . . . . . . . . . . . . . . . . . 67
Principle Five—Time . . . . . . . . . . . . . . . . . . . . . . . . . . . . . . . . . . . . 69
Principle Six—Rebalancing. . . . . . . . . . . . . . . . . . . . . . . . . . . . . . . . 71
Summary . . . . . . . . . . . . . . . . . . . . . . . . . . . . . . . . . . . . . . . . . . . . . . . 72

**Chapter 7**

LEARN TO UNDERSTAND YOUR INVESTMENT CHOICES. .73

Investment Vehicle Choices. . . . . . . . . . . . . . . . . . . . . . . . . . . . . . . . . . . 74
Types of Mutual Funds . . . . . . . . . . . . . . . . . . . . . . . . . . . . . . . . . . . . . . 74
Fixed-Income Funds . . . . . . . . . . . . . . . . . . . . . . . . . . . . . . . . . . . . . . . . 76
Equity Funds. . . . . . . . . . . . . . . . . . . . . . . . . . . . . . . . . . . . . . . . . . . . . . 78
International Equities Funds . . . . . . . . . . . . . . . . . . . . . . . . . . . . . . . . . 80
Summary. . . . . . . . . . . . . . . . . . . . . . . . . . . . . . . . . . . . . . . . . . . . . . . . . 80

**Chapter 8**

LEARN HOW TO DESIGN A WELL-BALANCED
INVESTMENT PORTFOLIO. . . . . . . . . . . . . . . . . . . . . . . . . . . . .83

Protecting Your Investment. . . . . . . . . . . . . . . . . . . . . . . . . . . . . . . . . . 84
How Aggressive Do You Need to Be? . . . . . . . . . . . . . . . . . . . . . . . . . 85
What Is a Reasonable Growth Rate of Return?. . . . . . . . . . . . . . . . . . 85
How Do You Measure the Risk of an Investment? . . . . . . . . . . . . . . . 86
Asset Mix Shift . . . . . . . . . . . . . . . . . . . . . . . . . . . . . . . . . . . . . . . . . . . 90
And Now—Putting It Together! . . . . . . . . . . . . . . . . . . . . . . . . . . . . . 91
Summary. . . . . . . . . . . . . . . . . . . . . . . . . . . . . . . . . . . . . . . . . . . . . . . . . 98

**Chapter 9**

LEARN THE RIGHT WAY TO GET YOUR MONEY OUT. . . . . .99

Accessing Your Funds While Still Working. . . . . . . . . . . . . . . . . . . . . 100
Take Out a Participant Loan. . . . . . . . . . . . . . . . . . . . . . . . . . . . . . . . . 100
Options Prior to Age 59½ or Actual Retirement Age. . . . . . . . . . . . . 104
Options After Age 59½ or Actual Retirement Age. . . . . . . . . . . . . . . 104
Type of Distributions . . . . . . . . . . . . . . . . . . . . . . . . . . . . . . . . . . . . . . 105
Summary. . . . . . . . . . . . . . . . . . . . . . . . . . . . . . . . . . . . . . . . . . . . . . . . . 107
Free Information . . . . . . . . . . . . . . . . . . . . . . . . . . . . . . . . . . . . . . . . . . 107

**Glossary** . . . . . . . . . . . . . . . . . . . . . . . . . . . . . . . . . . . . . . . . . . . . . . . 109

**Suggested Reading** . . . . . . . . . . . . . . . . . . . . . . . . . . . . . . . . . . . . . . 121

**About the Authors** . . . . . . . . . . . . . . . . . . . . . . . . . . . . . . . . . . . . . . 127

# How to Build, Protect and Maintain Your 401(k) Plan

## Strategies & Tactics

# Introduction

Y*ou will never have more money than you plan to have!* You could certainly end up with a little less, but never more. That's almost a universal law. Therefore, the goal of this booklet is to make sure that, at the very least, you end up with what you *plan* to have at retirement.

There are many types of tax-deferred retirement plans available. This booklet concentrates on 401(k) plans, one of the most prevalent and popular retirement programs. However, the principles outlined are applicable to all participant-directed retirement plans including 403(b), SEP, simple IRA, simple 401(k), or any other participant-directed investment plan. For the purposes of our discussion, we will use the 401(k) to represent all of them.

## Before We Get Started . . .

It is our firm belief that every employee has a responsibility to make his/her company as profitable as possible — to do something every day that will either save or make a buck for the company. The collective efforts of all the employees in a company, doing that on all the workdays of the year, can build great wealth. *And*, it's the employer's responsibility to then share that wealth in the form of increased employer contributions.

Before you read this, you probably thought it was none of your business what the worker beside you did: the guy making the deliveries, the installer, the woman running marketing. But from today on, you will know that every employee is a profit center for the company. Employees are either putting money directly into the employer's pocket — or taking money directly *out of* it. There is no middle ground.

If you're an employee, try to make your employer's business so profitable that your boss has to either give the profit to you or to Uncle Sam. Even a selfish employer would rather give it to you. Nobody wants to give it to Uncle Sam.

That's how free enterprise works, and that's how your 401(k) plan can work! You see, we're all in this together. When we all pull together, we can have the greatest 401(k) plan ever. Of course, there is one slight problem: *The building, protecting and investing of your 401(k) retirement plan is up to you.* Gone are the days of pension plans controlled by employers with inflation-adjusted benefits. It's **your** responsibility to understand how your 401(k) plan works. Technically . . .

> A 401(k) plan is a defined-contribution retirement plan that allows workers to save for retirement in accounts invested in equities and fixed-income securities. The contributions are made before tax, and any earnings on those contributions compound tax-free until distribution in retirement. The plan is sponsored by firms for their employees and, in recent years, these accounts have grown with such speed and popularity that they are displacing traditional defined-benefit pension plans.

These types of plans may be the only tax-sheltered vehicle available to the common, ordinary, working man or woman — and could be the only chance they have to break the paycheck-to-paycheck cycle most Americans live their lives by. Some participants have said, "I'm the first person in my family to ever save $10,000." Building up their 401(k) plans has changed these participants' outlook on money and the role it will play for the rest of their lives.

Think of your 401(k) as an empty bucket that you put money into, and the money is not taxable until you take it out at retirement. Since the bucket starts out empty, it's up to you to fill it. That is the purpose of this booklet — to show you how to fill your 401(k) bucket, help it grow, and learn the best ways to take your money out at retirement.

We tell people, "This may be the one chance in your life to become a capitalist. Don't miss it."

## Nine Building Blocks: How to Build, Protect and Maintain Your 401(k) Plan

The process for successfully building a strong 401(k) — and protecting these assets over time — can be broken down into nine specific steps, or "building blocks." Each step — or block — fits together with the others to create a solid program for guiding the plan along the path to greater wealth and financial security. In this booklet, each chapter outlines one of the nine steps and explains clearly how — if followed — any investor can build, protect and maintain a successful investment plan.

- **The first chapter advises you to learn what's in your Summary Plan Description (SPD).**
  Your plan is the cornerstone of your retirement, so, it's important that you learn every angle and how to work it in your favor. It doesn't help if you have a general knowledge of 401(k) plans, but don't understand the specific rules of your *own* plan.

- **Chapter Two helps you learn how to put money *into* y o u r plan.**
  It's possible that you aren't aware of rules affecting contributions to your specific plan. What are the eligibility requirements and vesting schedule? How much money you can put into your plan? What is the tax-free allowance or government subsidy? Since only you know exactly how each of these plan elements affect you, the more knowledge you have, the greater possibility you have of getting the full benefit of your plan.

- **Chapter Three urges you to learn how Employer Matching Funds can add money to your plan.**
  Matching funds are basically free money, and you would be crazy to turn away free money. That's what you're doing if your company offers a matching employer contribution and you're not putting in the amount necessary to receive the maximum matching funds. Find out the eligibility requirements and begin participating as soon as possible. Any delay is throwing money away!

- **Know the amount of risk you're willing to take, and learn to gauge it using the parameters outlined in Chapter Four.**
  Everybody is a long-term investor—until the market drops one percent or until you get your quarterly statement. What is your true tolerance for risk? Discover the answer in this section.

- **The fifth chapter helps you understand asset classes, so you can make more informed choices.**
  *Asset class* is a term frequently used, and as frequently misunderstood, in the investment world; but, asset classes are really nothing more than categories of various types of investments. We'll explain what they are, one by one, and explain how they work together.

- **The six principles of successful investing are highlighted in Chapter Six.**
  Six investment principles featured in this chapter will give you the highest possible probability for success. These principles work together to smooth out the roller-coaster ride associated with good and bad markets. Learn more about them to produce steady results.
  1. Dollar Cost Averaging
  2. Diversification
  3. Asset Allocation to Build a Portfolio
  4. Asset-Class Investing
  5. Time
  6. Rebalancing

- **Chapter Seven will help you understand all your investment choices, so you can make selections that meet your own investment needs and goals.**
  When you build an effectively diversified portfolio, you'll need to combine funds for each asset class. Your plan is required to provide a prospectus for each of these choices. Familiarize yourself with what is available, then ask questions to be certain you're getting the characteristics you require to meet your own risk/reward threshold.

- **Chapter Eight shows you how to design and structure a well-balanced investment portfolio.**
  Having your own personal investment plan for accumulating capital will help you set reasonable goals and manage your expectations for reaching them. Plus, it will help you not panic because

you "heard something" on the news, and stop you from defaulting to short-term moves, thereby, potentially missing out on gains that long-term investors enjoy with much less effort.

- **And finally, the last chapter will address the all important concept of knowing the *right* way to get your money out**
Because of tax implications and inflation, *how and when* you take money out of your plan could be more important than how you put it in. Learn the distribution rules, including any loan provisions. Learn liquidation strategies for your investments while they continue to grow, what to do when you change employers, and how to minimize the tax impact on distributions.

Step by step, "block by block," each chapter in this compact guide will clarify in simple terms the various elements that go into creating a robust portfolio that meets both immediate and long-term goals. Now — take control, and enjoy the ride!

▲ ▲ ▲ ▲ ▲ ▲

## Acknowledgement

We gratefully acknowledge and salute the thousands of 401(k) and 403(b) participants in plans designed and administered by The Rogers Companies and their employers who give their employees the finest program available so that they may succeed financially.

And we especially acknowledge the efforts of Rogers & Associates' staff—Joan Perry, QPA, Senior Vice President—Operations; Alice Frazier, QPA, Senior Vice President—Administration; and Kevin Combrink, QPA, Senior Vice President —Consulting.

In addition, we acknowledge the staff of Rogers Capital Management, Inc., and especially, Bill Harrell, Senior Vice President and Bill Rush, Senior Vice President/Operations without whom the investment education goals for thousands of participants could not be met.

Also, to Debbie Jones, our Executive Secretary, without whom our task would have been overwhelming.

And, finally, to Larry Chambers without whom our thoughts would not have conveyed the intended message, and Jaye Abbate and the team at Marketplace Books.

# Chapter 1

# LEARN WHAT'S IN YOUR SUMMARY PLAN DESCRIPTION (SPD)

Your plan is the cornerstone of your retirement; so, it's important that you learn every angle and how to work it in your favor. Not all plans are alike, so general knowledge of 401(k) plans isn't enough. In order to build, protect, and maintain your plan, it's necessary to take the time to know what your own plan says. And as a participant, it's your **right** to be knowledgeable.

You'll find it's not that hard to understand. All the features of a 401(k) — eligibility, benefits, rules, investments, and so on — are summarized in the SPD in a way that anyone can understand. It is intended to sum up the legalese in the plan in language intended for the layperson.

The Employee Retirement Income Security Act of 1974 (ERISA) requires that employees be given a copy of the SPD no later than 90 days after becoming a participant in the plan.

**If you haven't received a copy of the Summary Plan Description, request one. Read it.** Underline anything you don't understand. Most plan supervisors or HR persons want to be of assistance, but they can sometimes be confused themselves. Request that your company's plan representative explain in detail anything you find confusing. If you have a specific question, you have the right under ERISA to get it in writing. Ask the representative to show you in the summary where what he or she is telling you is correct.

Some people have their entire net worth tied up in plans without knowing how they work. This means that they may base their decisions on assumptions that are incorrect.

Some of the first points to answer are:
- What are the eligibility requirements?
- What are allowable contributions and their limits?
- What is the vesting schedule?
- What are the beneficiary rules?
- How do the distribution rules work?
- Are there loan provisions?

Since only you know exactly how each of these plan elements affects you, the more knowledge you have, the better chance of success you have.

Your employer has put this plan in place as a benefit for you. Unfortunately, plan administrators often give misinformation to employees. Even if your plan administrator gives you wrong information, you're still bound by your plan. The larger the company gets, the more likely it is that there will be some misinformation.

## Eligibility (Who Can Invest?)

Your plan may require a year of service or that you be at least 21 years of age — or both — before you are eligible to participate. This is primarily to lessen the impact of turnover within the plan, which occurs most frequently within the first year of employment. Most employers want to reward people who help make the company grow long term.

A year of service is calculated generally as a 12-month period, beginning on the first day of employment, during which an employee completes at least 1,000 hours of service. If the employee does not complete 1,000 hours of service during the initial eligibility computation period, the next period begins on the anniversary date of employment or, if provided in the plan, on the first day of the plan year during which the anniversary date falls. Years of service with a previous employer can qualify for eligibility and vesting if the successor employer maintains the previous employer's qualified plan.

A year of service includes periods of time such as vacation, holidays, illness, jury duty, and other specified instances during which no real work was performed, but the employee nonetheless received compensation.

## Vesting

Vesting is just another term for ownership. Any money that *you* put into a 401(k) is always 100 percent *vested*. Vesting schedules require an employee to remain employed by the sponsor and to participate in the plan for a certain period of time in order to own 100 percent of the employer's matching contributions.

The vesting clock starts ticking the day you are employed whether or not you are enrolled in the plan. In applying these vesting rules, know how your company's plan defines a *year of service*, which can be a calendar year, a plan year, or any period consisting of 12 consecutive months during which the participant has completed 1,000 or more hours of service. Internal Revenue Code section 411 specifies permissible vesting schedules that establish limits on the amount of time that a plan may require an employee to vest in his or her benefits.

> **The two most common types of vesting are *graded* vesting and *cliff* vesting.**

A recent survey reveals that as an incentive to keep employees participating on a long-term basis, 67 percent of employers have set up vesting schedules that require employees to participate in the plan for a certain number of years before qualifying for full ownership of the company's matching contribution.

The two most common types of vesting are *graded* vesting and *cliff* vesting.

### Graded Vesting

You own an increasing portion of any matched money contribution each year that you are employed with the company. If you are

## Example of Four-Year Graded Vesting

| Years of Service | Cumulative % Earned |
|---|---|
| 1 | 25% |
| 2 | 50% |
| 3 | 75% |
| 4 | 100% |

## Example of Three-Year Cliff Vesting

| Years of Service | Vested % |
|---|---|
| 1 | 0% |
| 2 | 0% |
| 3 | 100% |

participating in a four-year graded plan, you vest or own 25% of the company money every year (25% x 4 years = 100%). In a five-year graded plan, you own 20 percent per year. If you leave your employment before you are fully vested, you are entitled to the current vesting percentage of the matched monies.

A graded vesting schedule cannot exceed six years.

### Cliff Vesting

You own nothing until a certain period of time has passed. If you leave before you are fully vested, you get nothing. As you can see, there is a big incentive to hang in there until you are vested. Cliff vesting is most common in defined-benefit plans, but you will also find it in about 13 percent of 401(k) plans. Employers who use cliff vesting are required to vest you 100 percent after your third year of service.

**If you become disabled,** many plans will accelerate vesting on the employer contributions to 100 percent, but there's no law that states that they have to do so.

## What Happens in the Event of Your Death?

This may not be your favorite topic, but you need to make sure your beneficiary designations are correct. Every year people are unintentionally disinherited due to misunderstandings. You must plan for every contingency. Suppose, for instance, someone dies who had recently remarried:

Helen Roberts had $150,000 in savings, which she intended to leave to her children. She married and soon after died unexpectedly. Her brand-new husband inherited her money, instead of her children. Helen had not known that federal law stipulates that if someone remarries, their spouse automatically becomes their beneficiary, unless the spouse, after marriage, waives the right to be the sole beneficiary.

Another all-too-common occurrence is in the event of divorce when the beneficiary designation hasn't been changed, and the former spouse is still going to get the money. **Important: Only a spouse can waive a spousal benefit.**

Not every case is so straight forward. Look at this example of a single mother of two young children killed in a car accident. The young mother had worked for a very successful firm, and had made extensive contributions, worth around $100,000. She had named her mother as her beneficiary, knowing that if something happened to her, her mother would raise the grandchildren. The grandmother would have done exactly that, but about six weeks later, she was diagnosed with an aggressive form of bone cancer, and died only one month after the diagnosis.

The deceased young woman had a brother and a sister who, legally, were next in line for the money, before the children. When it was explained to them that their sister had left the money to their mother so she could take care of the children, they were understanding and agreed that the money rightfully belonged to the children. They verbally consented to waive their rights to their sister's money. But when they went home and talked with their respective spouses, things

> **You need to make sure your beneficiary designations are correct. Every year people are unintentionally disinherited due to misunderstandings. You must plan for every contingency.**

changed. The spouses convinced the brother and sister that they shouldn't relinquish the money.

So, even though she had good intentions, the single mom unintentionally disinherited her own children.

## How Are the Funds Paid to Your Beneficiary?

There are probably different distribution options available to your beneficiary. Discuss with your spouse, or other beneficiary, the most advantageous way to withdraw the money at your death, or to defer it to the future. Obviously, like any other plan, this would be subject to change based on the liquidity needs of your family.

## When and Where to Get Help

You are going to be the builder of your own portfolio. It's not that hard, with knowledge. Without knowledge, it's impossible. Set up a program that you can stick with. Here are the things you need:

1. a strategy;
2. a way to implement the strategy;
3. and somebody to make sure you don't shoot yourself in the foot.

### Ask for Help

Someone or some group or some company sold your employer on your 401(k) plan. They are responsible for educating you about the investment choices they are offering. Beyond that, you must know how to utilize those investments to build a diversified portfolio that reflects your risk tolerance and goals. Investment education is your right, so ask that someone be available to assist you. Ask your 401(k) coordinator to take the lead in setting up appropriate in-person or phone meetings.

If your plan's investment advisors are not assisting participants, then there are hundreds of firms that are willing and able to do so. That's what makes them competitive. Let your employer know if you aren't getting the help you need. Under ERISA 404(c), it is in the employers' best interest to see that you, the participant, are educated in the investment choices offered and how to use them.

It's what you don't know that can absolutely kill you — a little bit of knowledge is more dangerous than no knowledge. Keep asking for help until continuing investment education is available consistently from a professional. Do not seek out the opinions of non-professionals such as family, friends or acquaintances. They love to give opinions, but generally have limited knowledge to be of use.

The highest probability of success comes from:

- Getting help
- Understanding the plan rules
- Understanding the different investments
- Choosing a way to implement your strategy

## Summary

- Not all plans are alike.
- Take the time to understand how your plan works.
- Make sure your beneficiary designations reflect your intentions.
- Ask for help

Next, let's review the rules affecting your contributions to your specific plan.

# Chapter 2

# LEARN HOW TO PUT MONEY INTO YOUR PLAN

Automatic payroll deductions are probably the optimum way to save, psychologically removing any temptation or need for an arbitrary decision each time you get money about whether or not, and how much, to save. There may be limitations affecting contributions to your specific plan.

There is no longer a limit of 25 percent of an employee's salary when funding a 401(k) plan. Now even low-income earners can contribute the full $12,000-$15,000 — if they can swing it. Contributions outside your salary deduction may not be permitted. Be certain you know exactly how much, when and from where you can contribute annually to your plan. And, find out the parameters of any employer matching contributions, to make sure you take full advantage of this free money.

The best way to get money into your plan is through a regular payroll deduction in the same amount every month. This is called "dollar cost averaging". Automatic dollar cost averaging takes the fluctuations out of the market. So, some months this money will be invested when the markets are down, and some months you'll invest when the markets are up. Over time, you could end up owning more shares at a lower price than if you had invested all your money at once. And, because your retirement account is growing through tax-deferred compounding, the more you put away, the faster it will grow. This will be discussed in more detail in Chapter Five.

## How Your Contributions Get Invested

The 401(k) contribution process begins with the payroll department. The payroll department generally reports year-to-date contributions along with the current deductions from gross wages on employee pay stubs. This is a convenient way to track how frequently and how much you are contributing to your 401(k).

The plan sponsor (employer) has a legal obligation to make sure your 401(k) plan operates according to the law. This means that they can't collect money out of your paycheck and leave town with it, use it for other purposes, or let it sit around. As soon as it's administratively feasible, the money withheld from your paycheck must go to the designated retirement fund. In no event, can it be later than 15 business days after the end of the month in which the money comes out of the employee's paycheck. Deductions such as FICA and income tax withholding have to be transmitted to the IRS within three business days. Employers are supposed to notify their employees if they hold onto these funds for any reason.

Before your contributions can be deposited in the trust, your employer must perform a number of administrative activities for every employee in the plan, such as making sure the right percentage was deducted, calculating any match, in some cases segregating your money to be invested according to your wishes, and making sure there are no IRS or other attachments first in line on your money.

Let's say that your employer goes bankrupt between deducting your contribution and putting it into the trust. Because this money is still technically wages, it should revert to you. Creditors of the company cannot attach your wages, only assets of the company. When your money reaches the trust, it becomes safe from any troubles or temptations that might beset your employer.

The trustee then invests this money according to your direction. The trust is a legal entity, charged with the responsibility of safeguarding your money. Trustees are required by law to protect your money, invest it according to your instructions, and are responsible for keeping track of the plan's assets as a whole — but the trustee is *not* the plan administrator.

The trustee has a fiduciary responsibility to make sure that the mutual funds offered for investment are suitable for you and your beneficiaries. Many of these investment choices wouldn't be available at a retail level to small investors. A trustee only makes a distribution to a terminated participant, a retiree, or a beneficiary when instructed to do so by the plan administrator. Anyone who handles plan assets must be bonded (have insurance to indemnify the plan in case of mistake or in case of fraud). If the trustee is an individual, an officer of your company, for example, then he or she must be bonded.

In the case of a participant-directed plan, the trustee exercises no judgment on how you elect to invest your 401(k) money. The money is invested according to the instructions you have given. The employer, the plan administrator, the trustee and the mutual fund do not offer any guarantees on the return you'll get on your money. All the employer, plan administrator and trustee are doing is making sure that the money that comes out of your check goes to the right investment account.

## Taking Advantage of Pre-Tax Dollars

All 401(k) plans, by definition, are CODAs. The term CODA (cash or deferred arrangement) refers to whether you want to reduce your salary for the 401(k) or not. Do you want your cash or are you going to defer some of it to the 401(k)? CODA refers precisely to the ability of eligible employees to elect a *contribution rate,* also known as deferral percentage or savings rate, up to an allowable maximum percentage of their compensation, to be contributed to the plan by the employer on their behalf. The amount contributed to the plan under the CODA is called an *elective contribution.*

These elective contributions and the earnings on those contributions are not generally subject to income taxes, federal or state, until you withdraw those funds from the 401(k). (Check with your own state to see how the 401(k) affects your income tax.) While employed, a 10-percent penalty tax may be imposed if you withdraw the funds prior to age 59½. For participants who have separated from service (terminated employment), the 10 percent penalty only applies if you receive a distribution prior to age 55. If you terminate employment and withdraw funds after age 55, there is no penalty tax.

Your contributions will be deducted from your paycheck every pay period. For example, if you gross $3,000 per month and you've selected a 10 percent contribution rate, you're putting $300 a month ($3,000 x 10% = $300) into your 401(k) account. Most companies track the amount that you have contributed on your paycheck. You can usually change your contribution rate any time you want.

Recently enacted changes in laws governing 401(k) plans provide dramatically higher contribution limits and even catch-up options that can make up for poor savings habits or simply help to maximize tax deferral and wealth accumulation. This increased limit for 2004 is $13,000 and will continue to increase at the rate of $1,000 per year through the year 2006, when it will be $15,000. In addition, if you are 50 years of age or older, you can make a graduated *catch-up* contribution of $3,000 beginning in the tax year 2004, increasing in increments of $1000 per year, up to $5000 in 2006.

> **Recently enacted changes in laws governing 401(k) plans provide dramatically higher contribution limits and even catch-up options that can make up for poor savings habits or simply help to maximize tax deferral and wealth accumulation.**

This new law also enhanced portability, or transferability, of retirement accounts beginning in the 2002 tax year. It simplifies rollovers between various tax-shelter plans; for example, you now have the right to roll over regular pretax IRA account balances. There's no longer any reason to have separate regular IRA accounts and rollover IRA accounts and 401(k) plans — they can be commingled. A loan provision in your 401(k) could be an additional incentive to combine all your retirement funds, since you can't take a loan against an IRA.

## Getting Started

If you've never been a saver, start by contributing the minimum possible—even if it's just one percent of your paycheck to your 401(k). That's it. You won't notice any difference in your paycheck, but the important thing is that you've gotten started. The longest journey starts with a single step. It doesn't matter how small: just do it. Don't use dollar amounts; use percentages. If you have a fixed-dollar amount and you only work three days one week, it could wreck your whole paycheck. But if you have a short week, and you're contributing a percentage, the amount you contribute will be less. If you make more money, you'll be contributing a little more. Hourly workers should never set up dollar amount contributions, always percents. If you contribute a specific percent to your 401(k) plan, say, 6 percent, that means that out of every $100 you earn, $6.00 is put into your 401(k). If you make $500, six percent would be a $30 deduction.

Increase your contributions automatically. After a few months, increase your contribution by just one percent. When you're used to that, raise it one percent more.

What happens if you toss a frog into boiling water? It will jump out. But if you put that frog into lukewarm water and gradually increase the temperature, the frog will remain in the water until it boils.

If we throw non-savers and non-investors into a symbolic "pot of boiling water" where they are required to save a substantial amount —they'll hop out. But if we start them off with something they hardly notice and gradually increase them, they'll find themselves saving six to ten percent of their income, painlessly.

> **If you've never been a saver, start by contributing the minimum possible—even if it's just one percent of your paycheck to your 401(k). That's it.**

Your first job is to become a saver. Our job is to educate you on how next to become an investor.

**Try this exercise:**

1. Take your average week's contribution and convert that to a percentage of your pay: _____ percent

2. Figure out how much monthly income you want to have when you retire. For instance, you may want to retire on as much as you're making at the time you retire. If you're making $3,000 a month now, but expect to be making $6,000 a month by retirement age, write that down: $_____

3. Figure out how much money you will need to accumulate to provide that income. A rule of thumb is that for every $1000, you'll need to save $100,000. In the example of $6000, you're going to need $600,000 or $700,000 to match your salary. See why you must do this?

You can estimate that Social Security will pay you between $700 and $1500 a month depending on how much you put in. So you'll still have to come up with $5000 a month. If you're smart, you won't even plan for Social Security; you'll just do it all on your own. Then if you do get Social Security, it will be a bonus.

This money has to last you the rest of your life. There are two ways to make it happen. One way is to liquidate the principal as you go; or you will need to accumulate more money if you want to preserve your principal and live off only the earnings and pass any remainder on to your family.

You need to consider both the interest rate your investment can earn and your time horizon. An aggressive investor can plan for perhaps eight percent. For example, if you want $600,000 in 20 years, you will have to accumulate an average of $30,000 a year. You may not be able to save $30,000 a year— but you can't just put in $50 a month and think you're going to be okay for retirement.

# Exponential Growth Through Compounding

The acceleration of wealth accumulation through compounding is a major selling point for participating in a 401(k). That is, you earn on the cumulative amount of your *contributions* AND your *tax savings* AND on the *earnings* on your investments.

This chart below (Figure 2.1) will show you how much you'd need to contribute monthly, the number of years until retirement, and the rates of return you'd need to have a million dollars at retirement. Yes—accumulating a million dollars by retirement is not an impossible goal.

## Figure 2.1 WANT A MILLION?
## IT'S NOT IMPOSSIBLE!

When making your contribution there are only three basic variables an investor needs to grapple with. These are:

**1** **How long before you retire?** Now look along the top row for the number of years before you retire. (Years to retire)

**2** **The rate you need to make in your 401(k) plan.** Look down the left side for the rate of return you'd need to shoot for to make a million. (Rate of return you need)

**3** **How much $ do you need to contribute?** The intersecting box is the amount you'd have to set aside each month. (Your contribution)

| Rate of Return | NUMBER OF YEARS TO RETIREMENT | | | | | | | |
|---|---|---|---|---|---|---|---|---|
| | 15 | 20 | 25 | 30 | 35 | 40 | 45 | 50 |
| 5% | $3.7K | $2.4K | $1.7K | $1.2K | $880 | $655 | $493 | $375 |
| 6% | $3.4K | $2.2K | $1.4K | $996 | $702 | $502 | $363 | $264 |
| 7% | $3.2K | $1.9K | $1.2K | $820 | $555 | $381 | $264 | $184 |
| 8% | $2.9K | $1.7K | $1.1K | $671 | $436 | $286 | $190 | $126 |
| 9% | $2.6K | $1.5K | $892 | $546 | $340 | $214 | $135 | $86 |
| 10% | $2.4K | $1.3K | $754 | $442 | $263 | $158 | $95 | $58 |
| 11% | $2.2K | $1.2K | $634 | $357 | $203 | $116 | $67 | $39 |
| 12% | $2.0K | $1.0K | $532 | $286 | $156 | $85 | $47 | $26 |
| 13% | $1.8K | $882 | $445 | $229 | $119 | $62 | $32 | $17 |
| 14% | $1.7K | $769 | $371 | $182 | $90 | $45 | $22 | $11 |
| | **Monthly contribution needed to reach $1 million, (assuming monthly compounding).** | | | | | | | |

The last word on the subject is this: Stay with your 401(k) until you have maxed out your yearly plan limit or tax-deferral limit, as well as any catch-up contributions!

## Summary

- Automatic dollar cost averaging is the best way get money in your plan.
- Have a systematic plan to increase your contributions.
- The acceleration of pre-tax wealth accumulation through compounding is important to understand.

Next we will explore how to use your Employer Matching Contributions.

*Chapter 3*

# LEARN HOW EMPLOYER MATCHING FUNDS CAN ADD MONEY TO YOUR PLAN

The most unique aspect of 401(k) plans is that they allow companies to match employee contributions, up to a legally designated amount. This means your employer can actually make a contribution — usually in the form of "matching funds" — into *your* plan. This is FREE money! No matter what percentage your employer agrees to match and contribute — it's still free money. Do NOT pass it up! If you're eligible, sign up right away — don't delay! If you're not eligible, learn about the plan and your investment options and determine how much you should be saving to reach your retirement goal. On average, 401(k) participants funnel only around 6.7 percent of each paycheck into their plans.

There are various matching contributions. Your employer might offer a 25-percent match for every dollar you put in, so that for every $100, you get $25. Or it could be 150-percent match. In other words, you put in $1.00 and the employer puts in $1.50. Some plans have a fixed match with a formula and others are discretionary. Employers sponsoring a discretionary profit-sharing plan can put in from year-to-year whatever they wish to. A discretionary match can be very beneficial for the employee when the employer operates in good faith. In bad years, there may not be any match, but in good years, there should be a healthy match. By the time you know if the company has had a good year, it's too late. So put your money in, regardless.

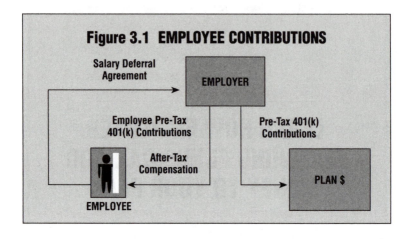

Figure 3.1 EMPLOYEE CONTRIBUTIONS

This might seem obvious, but you can't fully appreciate how important your contributions are until you see the consequences of not fully funding your 401(k). A few extra dollars going into your 401(k), now, means a whole lot extra coming out.

If you only get the tax advantage from Uncle Sam, it's still a great deal. But with the employer making contributions in the form of match or profit sharing contributions, that makes your accumulation dynamic. In rare cases, in order to help employees, companies will make contributions for all employees, even those not personally contributing themselves.

According to the Employee Benefit Research Institute's 2000 *Survey of Defined-Contribution Plans*, about 84 percent of companies that provide 401(k) plans also offer to match employees' contributions at some level. The most common match is 3 percent, or 50 cents, on each dollar the employee contributes, up to a maximum of 6 percent of that employee's compensation. This 3-percent match rate (50% of 6% = 3%) is found in many 401(k) plans, but a fair number of employers offer matches of 100 percent or even higher. That means when you put in a dollar, they put in at least a dollar.

## Read Your Plan's Fine Print

Since these matched contributions are appearing more as part of the overall compensation package, the 401(k) plan's design is critical in maximizing the value of a company's human-resource dollar. Take the time to study your company's Summary Plan Description (*see* Building Block One). See if it specifies that your company's 401(k) has a *nondiscretionary* (mandatory) match; that means that the plan sponsor *must* make a contribution. Discretionary matches are usually based upon the company being profitable.

> **It's to your benefit to check out the definition of *compensation* in your SPD to determine the types of pay that will be matched.**

Also, it's to your benefit to check out the definition of *compensation* in your SPD to determine the types of pay that will be matched. Regular pay, such as salary or hourly pay, plus overtime, are the most common definitions. But compensation could also include commissions, bonuses, shift differentials, or special awards. Since matched funds have a ceiling of a specified percentage of your compensation, you want to be sure you're using the highest total in your computation. Increase your contribution accordingly to receive the full benefit of any matched money.

Learn how often and when matched money is deposited into your account. Many plans match your account only if you're still employed on specific dates — say, December 31, the last day of the year. You won't consider yourself very smart if you leave the company on December 29, only to find out that you were two days short of receiving the next quarterly, semiannual, or annual match contribution.

## Matching in Company Stock

In many of the large plans (companies with thousands of employees), all or part of the employer's matched contribution is in the form of company stock. The belief is that employees who own shares in their company have a certain pride of ownership, or interest in the company's well–being. And it demonstrates management's good faith in the company's future.

> **Unlike defined benefit or pension plans, 401(k) contribution plans are *not* required by law to *diversify* their holdings — although there is now a rush to do that.**

The bull market of the past 20 years masked the problems associated with owning company stock inside your 401(k) plan. As long as the market was going up, most companies' stocks soared in value along with 401(k) account balances, and employees were happy to get *free* shares of company stock contributed to their long-term retirement plan. Whether out of loyalty, ignorance, or convenience, more and more employees also opted to direct all, or a large percentage, of their own contributions to be invested in company stock. According to the Profit–Sharing 401(k) Council of America, the single largest investment in 401(k) plans is employer's stock — 39 percent of total assets. This high percentage of concentration and *overweighting* in a single equity resulted in an imprudent exposure to volatility and business risk.

When, in 2001, many publicly held companies dropped 40 to 60 percent of their value, 401(k) portfolios that weren't diversified over different asset classes suffered severe losses. Unlike defined benefit or pension plans, 401(k) contribution plans are *not* required by law to *diversify* their holdings — although there is now a rush to do that.

What happened at Enron is a glaring example of overweighting in one stock. About 63 percent of the employees' retirement money was invested in Enron stock. When Enron imploded, some $1 billion of savings disappeared. Now everyone is scrutinizing their portfolios to see if they are overweight in one company and, to the extent they are, they're going to be shuffling assets around to reduce that exposure.

Of course, there are always two sides to every story. On one side of this issue are situations like the downfall of Enron, Global Crossing, or Lucent Technology. On the opposite side are the companies such as General Electric, Dell, Home Depot, and Microsoft, whose value is up hundreds, if not thousands, of percent over the last 10 years. For instance, $10,000 of Microsoft stock acquired in 1986 would be worth $5 million today!

A match in the form of company stock is *not* necessarily a bad thing. For every negative story related to company stock, a good one can be found. There's nothing wrong with owning company stock, as long as you accept the volatility.

## Company Stock and Your Job

Most employees don't realize that they are placing a whopper of a bet on their employer when their primary income depends on the company, their benefits depend on it, and all their 401(k) assets also depend on the value of its stock. The future security and value of each of these is tied together. Many of the companies whose shares have dropped 50 percent in value over the last 36 months have also downsized. So, not only did some participants lose significant value in their retirement plans, many lost their income and benefits as well.

In order to recover from a 50 percent loss, a 100 percent gain must occur. And, that's possible over time. But, if you're 59 years old and planning to retire and 60 percent of your 401(k) plan assets were in Enron, you're sunk. You don't have the time to make up for losses that you sustained.

## Correct Through Diversification

The way to correct an overweighting in company stock is to diversify a percentage of

**Figure 3.2
REGAINING YOUR LOSS**

| If you lose this much | You'll need to earn this much to break even |
|---|---|
| 10% | 11% |
| 20% | 25% |
| 30% | 43% |
| 40% | 67% |
| 50% | 100% |
| 60% | 150% |
| 70% | 233% |
| 80% | 400% |
| 90% | 900% |

your 401(k) assets into some other investment that tends to move dissimilarly to your company stock. This may seem like common sense, but, in fact, it was a dramatic breakthrough in investment methodology when Harry Markowitz developed his Nobel Prize-winning theory back in the 1950s.

> **If you leave your company and you have shares of company stock in your 401(k) plan, you can either transfer the stock to an IRA, or liquidate the stock and transfer the proceeds to your new 401(k) plan, or take the stock at that time.**

Markowitz demonstrated that, to the extent that securities in a portfolio do *not* move in concert with each other, their individual risks could be effectively diversified away.

If you leave your company and you have shares of company stock in your 401(k) plan, you can either transfer the stock to an IRA, or liquidate the stock and transfer it to your new 401(k) plan, or take the stock at that time. If you take the stock, you will pay ordinary income tax on the stock's "basis" (it's cost at the time contributed, not its appreciated value). The new capital gains tax rates often make it better to pay ordinary income tax on your stock's basis now and sell it later, when you will be taxed at a 15 percent rate, or possibly lower, depending on your income. This beats paying the ordinary income tax rate of up to 35 percent. If you elect to not take the stock, there will be no tax at that time, but you will pay ordinary tax on the full value of the stock when it is later distributed.

Company stock inside your 401(k):

- If you have the option to choose between a matching contribution of stock or cash, choose cash — for its liquidity as well as your ability to direct its investment. (Remember: you are already betting your wages on the future of your employer, and you may also be participating in their stock-option plan!)

- If your plan sponsor requires that company stock must be held for a certain period, even after it is fully vested inside the plan, *rebalance* your percentage of stock ownership in your overall 401(k) as soon as possible.

- Evaluate your tax options concerning company stock if you leave your employer — whether you change jobs or retire.

## Summary

- Don't turn down free money! Understand the parameters of your company match.

- Know what types of pay will be matched.

- Be sure you are diversified when the match is company stock.

When investing for a specific return, do you know how much risk you must take? The next Building Block will answer that question.

# Chapter 4

# LEARN HOW MUCH RISK YOU SHOULD TAKE

## Everybody Is a Long-Term Investor — Until They Get Their Quarterly Statement

We know how to help everyone make money; however, only a fraction of people can stick with the program because of the inherent volatility. For some investors, the most important thing is to know that they're not going to lose their principal. Unfortunately, there are only a few types of investments that are guaranteed not to lose principal, and with those, your earnings are just going to keep up with inflation. It's the oldest rule in investing: No risk, no reward.

If you are absolutely terrified to be in the market, then you don't have any business being in stock mutual funds in the first place. You'll have to settle for money-market instruments. There's no shame in that; the stock market doesn't suit everyone's constitution.

Or you could be just partially in the market; perhaps 20 percent, or 40 percent in the market and the rest in fixed income, such as money markets. Some 401(k)s have guaranteed investment accounts or bond funds. Don't hesitate to use one of those instruments; at the same time, realize that you're not going to make a lot of money.

We want to insure your investment strategy is designed to reflect your personal risk tolerance. Risk tolerance is your capacity to

> **Your risk tolerance is one of the most critical components for setting up your portfolio mix.**

tolerate unfavorable conditions, during the time period you hold your investments, without making changes. It has to do with how much you can lose and not be tempted to abandon your investment program.

Determining risk tolerance is more challenging than filling out a risk tolerance questionnaire because it is difficult to measure, and changes over time. Reflecting on your past, and looking at some of the major decisions you've made over your lifetime, can help in assessing your risk tolerance. What motivated you to make those decisions?

Your risk tolerance is one of the most critical components for setting up your portfolio mix. If a participant doesn't want to lose more than 10 percent, then he would be a candidate for a 60/40 portfolio.

If he can't withstand declines of more than five percent, he'd better be somewhere in the 30/70 to 40/60 portfolio mix. Or if he can't withstand a decline of more than 15 percent, he'd better have a truly diversified portfolio. If he's not diversified, all bets are off. Some equity portfolios have lost 50 percent and more in the 2000-2002 years because they were not truly diversified. There's no limit to what you can lose if you're not diversified.

People don't like to lose money, and their anxiety about doing so can cause them to make unwise decisions. If that's the case, a more aggressive portfolio is not an appropriate choice.

## Managing Risk

Start with less risk. If you're thinking, *I think I could go aggressive, but I'm not sure*, then don't. Before 2000, participants who were conservative by nature were in very aggressive investment portfolios because stock returns had been excellent for several years. In fact, many participants believed that the stock market "goes up every year." WRONG!!

If you're increasing risk, it's almost never to your detriment. If you start with a 60/40 and later decide, "I can take more risk — my portfolio hardly went down at all in these three bad years," then that's not going to hurt you. But if you go the other way, you are practically guaranteed to realize a loss. If someone is tempted to move from an aggressive to a less aggressive portfolio, it's because of loss. Period.

However, if you just woke up to the fact that you have only a few years left until retirement and there is a huge gap between your assets and the amount of money you will need, you are going to have to increase your investment risk to get higher expected returns. This may be opposite from the advice you've been reading in other books. But, aside from greatly increasing the amount you're saving, how else can you make up for lost time?

You can start by identifying all the known variables, such as how much you currently have saved in all your asset pools, the size and frequency of your contributions, the amount of matches, investment allocations, and how much time you have before retirement.

Then, compare your long-term dollar needs with your portfolio performance and evaluate the probability of achieving those goals. In most cases, this evaluation will indicate a shortfall or a gap. At this point, your chances for success in achieving your financial goals are based solely on your current asset allocation and investment strategy.

Next, determine the maximum risk exposure you feel comfortable with. This will impact the probability of reaching your target retirement financial goals. If you are too conservative, that

> Determine the maximum risk exposure you feel comfortable with. . . . You must make a decision between accepting the downside of volatility and increased risk versus the promise of a higher probability of success.

probability will decrease. You must make a decision between accepting the downside of volatility and increased risk versus the promise of a higher probability of success. Then, after you have determined the amount of risk you are willing to assume, you must attempt to solve for unknown variables, such as future capital market returns. The focus is on what is reliably predictable. Look at the stock market over different time periods, and then adjust your allocation to meet your future risk tolerances. This is where most participants stop, because they don't know how much of an adjustment to make. You may need the help of an advisor or planner.

> **You have to think *not* in terms of how much you are willing to make, but how much you are willing to *lose*.**

If you have a long time horizon, you can do things more conservatively because time is on your side. But, if you discover that you still have a large gap, you may have to follow more aggressive strategies, such as concentrating more in equity investments, increasing your contributions, extending the age at which you wish to retire, and investing outside your 401(k) plan. Unfortunately, most people have lifestyle wants and needs that far exceed a reasonable growth rate of return inside their 401(k) plans. Again, you have to think *not* in terms of how much you are willing to make, but how much you are willing to *lose.*

## What Is Your Tolerance for Risk?

### The Lifeboat Drill

The most important thing about the lifeboat drill is that it's visual, and we are very visual beings. We react better to things we can see.

Assume for a moment that you have invested all of your money (we'll use $10,000 for simplicity). In the first quarter, your investment goes up three percent. You feel pretty good, right? In the next quarter, it goes up two percent. You're feeling even better. But what if your money starts to decline? Your ship is taking on water — how low in the water will you let the boat sink before you abandon ship and get in the lifeboat?

Let's say your quarterly statement shows you that your $10,000 has become $9700. Are you still on board? The next quarter, you're down to $9400. Then it drops to $9200. How are you feeling now? Are you still okay with doing nothing or are you getting your lifeboat ready? The following quarter, it drops to $9000. Let's assume no action is taken and it goes down further: to $8500, $7700, $6500, and eventually to $5000. At what point do you want to "jump ship"?

You might be willing to endure a three-percent decline; you probably aren't very willing to sit still at ten percent; and if you feel alone and emotional at a fifteen percent drop, you'll want out. It's fear that gets someone out of the market.

What's interesting is that most investors are willing to accept a greater *percentage* amount when it isn't related to a specific *dollar* amount:

## Figure 4.1 LIFEBOAT DRILL

| Potential Quarterly Decline | Original Investment $10,000 | Loss in Dollar Amounts |
|:---:|:---:|:---:|
| (3%) | $9700 | -$ 300 |
| (7%) | $9300 | -$ 700 |
| (10%) | $9000 | -$1000 |
| (15%) | $8500 | -$1500 |
| (23%) | $7700 | -$2300 |

Most surprising are people who have portfolios invested for maximum growth in very aggressive funds, but indicate they are willing to take only a 12 to 13 percent decline in their investment. Clearly, something is out of whack. Either they must be able to accept more decline, or they're invested completely inappropriately.

The biggest mistake you can make is to go beyond your risk tolerance, your threshold of comfort. You may panic, jump ship, and get in the lifeboat, and then not make your destination because you're floating in the middle of the ocean waiting to be rescued. And you watch the ship, which is doing fine, as it picks up steam and leaves you afloat. If you bailed out of equity mutual funds at the end of March 2003, you missed an average 20-percent return for the next quarter. You just saw your ship sail away.

## Summary

- Understand the relationship of risk to investment rewards.
- Learn how to balance risk.
- Determine your true risk tolerance threshold.

Now let's discuss asset classes, the subject of Building Block Five.

*Chapter 5*

# LEARN ABOUT THE VARIOUS ASSET CLASSES

## What Are Asset Classes?

*A*sset *class* is a term frequently used in the investment world to refer to a *category* of investment.

You're probably familiar with equity asset classes and fixed-income asset classes—the two main asset classes. For the purpose of our discussion, we are going to divide them into the following:

- Cash/Money Market
- Bonds
- U.S. Large-Growth Companies
- S&P 500
- U.S. Large-Value Companies
- U.S. Small-Growth Companies
- U.S. Small-Value Companies
- International Large Companies
- International Small Companies

These are listed from the safest to the most risky, but as you will discover, there is no absolute ranking of risk in the equity market.

## Cash

The first asset class called "cash" includes money-market funds, which are made up of T-Bills, Certificates of Deposit, and commercial paper. These are called cash because the NAV (net asset value) is always one dollar; in other words, the price doesn't fluctuate.

Few people understand that when their holdings are in cash, they're invested in an asset class.

## Bonds

Also called fixed-income, this asset class is divided into two main groups: stable bonds such as U.S. Government, **AAA** corporate bonds; and higher-yield bonds such as **bb** corporate bonds and "junk bonds."

> **We would never recommend junk bonds because they are actually unsecured loans of a company.**

We recommend only the first group. Within this category, we decide if we want long-term, intermediate, or shorter duration bonds. We recommend short-term bonds, meaning five years or less to maturity, because a short-duration fund will give you 94 percent of the return, without the long-term bond volatility. If you are in a long-term bond fund and interest rates move up, your fund can drop 25 percent in a day.

Never invest in junk bonds; it's not worth the risk. All you are doing is adding volatility without gaining the expected returns of a stock. We would never recommend junk bonds because they are actually unsecured loans of a company. Suppose a company goes bankrupt—that company's bondholders are secured and get paid before stockholders, but that is not the case with junk-bond owners. Those are usually general obligation instruments that are not backed up by any collateral, so you're last in line to get paid. When you think of bonds, think safety, not speculation.

## Equities

After cash and bonds, we subdivided asset classes into more specific categories distinguished by their unique characteristics. Equity, or stock, asset classes are often categorized according to the size of their market capitalization (number of outstanding shares multiplied by current stock price.)

### How It's Decided What Stocks Go Into an Asset Class

The way the academics built equity asset classes is quite involved. First, they took all the companies on the New York Stock Exchange, ranked them by size, and then divided them into ten deciles.

They designated the largest one tenth of the companies as Decile Number 1, including companies on the scale of General Electric or Chrysler. Decile Number 2 represented the next 10 percent graduating down in company size. Deciles 9 and 10 were the smallest companies, the bottom 20 percent in size. That's not an asset class yet, but it's part of an asset class.

Next, they looked at the NASDAQ and the American Stock Exchange, and they filled in the same capitalization requirements that were in Deciles 1 through 10. Deciles 1 through 5 qualify as large company stocks; small company stocks are in the 6 through 10 deciles.

The academic asset class of value stocks originally included every value stock, across all those same markets. They discovered that was too cumbersome, so they divided it into asset classes called large "value" and small "value." The same applies to "growth" and "international" equity asset classes.

## Large-Cap Growth

These are very large companies that are doing very well (they have a capitalization of approximately $10 billion or greater). This type of company usually has good sales, good prospects for the future, and good earnings.

## S & P 500 (Standard & Poors Index of the 500 Largest U.S. Stocks)

It seems there is a lot of confusion between asset classes and indexes, but there is a distinction. Asset classes are academically defined, whereas, an index is simply a numerical group of stocks. Indexes are commercial benchmarks. The S&P 500 is an index of 500 stocks. We also call it an equity asset class, even though it contains both large growth and large value stocks. It's well known and it gives people something to compare to.

> Asset classes for stocks are further refined into value and growth stock categories according to their potential total return over time.

## Large-Cap Value

These are large U.S. publicly traded companies that may be temporarily out of favor. They aren't doing well by any measurement. The companies are distressed economically.

## U.S. Small-Cap Growth

These are publicly traded U.S. smaller companies with a capitalization of less than $2 billion. They have good sales and good prospects for the future.

## U.S. Small-Cap Value

These are U.S. publicly traded smaller companies (with an average capitalization of less than $2 billion.) that aren't doing very well.

## International

The last two equity asset classes are international. This group generally comprises stocks of companies based outside the U.S. — from any part of the world with established free markets.

**Large** — International large companies that are doing very well, including growth to value stocks and everything in between.

**Small** — International small companies also include both growth and value stocks.

It's important to be clear about definitions that get tossed around. For instance, contrary to what many people believe, technology is not an asset class; it's a sector. Anyone who invests strictly in high tech and telecommunications (sector funds) is foregoing investment strategies for speculation in concentrated, high-risk sectors. Some would say anyone who does this is not only a speculator, but an outright gambler.

## Rate of Returns by Asset Class

Figure 5.1 on the following page shows how these seven equity asset classes have done individually compared to an entire diversified portfolio (3), over the last 30 years.

The asset classes are more precisely defined as follows:

**THE FIRST COLUMN: Small-value stocks** — Smallest 8 percent of market universe[1]* *based on total capitalization.* From that range, a value screen is given in which all issues' BtM (Book to Market Value) are calculated. In other words, small-value companies are very small in size, temporarily distressed and there are a huge number of them, over 2000.

Book-to-Market value is a ratio comparing the book value of a share of common stock with its market price. High BtM companies are companies in distress (and investors demand to be compensated for the perceived higher risk). Low book-to-market companies (like Microsoft and Wal-Mart) on average will do well, and, because they are so popular, investors are not compensated as well. Their cost of acquiring capital is less than other companies not in this group.

**THE SECOND COLUMN: Small-growth stocks**—Smallest 8 percent of the market universe[2] *using the lowest Book-to-Market ratio.* These are small companies, but they are doing very well compared to small-value companies. Their sales are good, price-to-

---

[1] Market Universe is defined as all stocks in the NYSE, AMEX, and NASDAQ. Source: Dimensional Fund Advisors Firm Profile & Returns Program.

[2] Ibid

## Figure 5.1 RATE OF RETURNS BY ASSET CLASS CHART

| Year | Small Value | Small Growth | Large Value | S&P 500 | Large Growth | Int'l. Small | Int'l. Large | Diversified Portfolio* |
|---|---|---|---|---|---|---|---|---|
| 1970 | 0.31 | (18.61) | 11.90 | 4.03 | (5.23) | 0.90 | (9.65) | (2.09) |
| 1971 | 14.40 | 23.49 | 9.44 | 14.32 | 23.60 | 68.25 | 59.87 | 26.45 |
| 1972 | 6.96 | 3.75 | 15.97 | 18.98 | 21.65 | 64.22 | 53.25 | 22.52 |
| 1973 | (26.01) | (39.10) | (2.75) | (14.67) | (20.34) | (13.68) | (22.34) | (20.06) |
| 1974 | (18.11) | (33.40) | (22.38) | (26.46) | (29.96) | (28.61) | (33.68) | (27.08) |
| 1975 | 54.45 | 63.17 | 51.92 | 37.21 | 35.66 | 49.86 | 65.26 | 50.30 |
| 1976 | 53.55 | 43.51 | 44.98 | 23.85 | 18.38 | 11.46 | 5.55 | 31.18 |
| 1977 | 21.81 | 20.32 | .75 | (7.18) | (9.13) | 74.08 | 40.61 | 15.72 |
| 1978 | 21.82 | 18.63 | 6.63 | 6.57 | 7.01 | 65.53 | 33.22 | 19.58 |
| 1979 | 37.95 | 47.26 | 23.779 | 18.42 | 20.69 | (0.78) | 2.11 | 23.83 |
| 1980 | 29.09 | 46.07 | 16.54 | 32.41 | 33.87 | 35.46 | 38.48 | 32.67 |
| 1981 | 10.54 | (4.09) | 11.23 | (4.91) | (7.90) | (4.65) | 0.86 | 0.40 |
| 1982 | 37.66 | 25.99 | 27.35 | 21.41 | 17.60 | 0.82 | 5.22 | 21.41 |
| 1983 | 44.22 | 26.92 | 26.77 | 22.51 | 16.23 | 32.40 | 22.23 | 27.33 |
| 1984 | 5.08 | (8.87) | 14.07 | 6.27 | (1.07) | 10.08 | 11.39 | 4.62 |
| 1985 | 34.73 | 28.51 | 29.46 | 32.17 | 31.45 | 60.11 | 48.28 | 35.85 |
| 1986 | 16.86 | 5.82 | 20.36 | 18.47 | 13.70 | 50.10 | 59.95 | 23.04 |
| 1987 | (6.30) | (10.00) | 2.32 | 5.23 | 6.40 | 70.55 | 41.43 | 10.82 |
| 1988 | 28.84 | 20.46 | 24.64 | 16.81 | 12.82 | 26.01 | 24.81 | 2.165 |
| 1989 | 19.69 | 19.09 | 28.35 | 31.49 | 31.52 | 29.34 | 14.67 | 25.22 |
| 1990 | (20.81) | (18.13) | (13.94) | (3.17) | 1.43 | (16.77) | (18.38) | (12.25) |
| 1991 | 39.37 | 52.11 | 29.82 | 30.55 | 41.14 | 7.05 | 13.95 | 32.98 |
| 1992 | 29.86 | 11.23 | 21.16 | 7.67 | 7.14 | (18.37) | (9.44) | 9.55 |
| 1993 | 22.56 | 14.04 | 21.16 | 9.99 | 2.01 | 33.49 | 36.44 | 18.15 |
| 1994 | (0.95) | (2.88) | (4.57) | 1.31 | 1.47 | 12.42 | 7.63 | 1.11 |
| 1995 | 29.24 | 31.28 | 37.19 | 37.43 | 37.92 | 0.48 | 13.72 | 29.11 |
| 1996 | 21.36 | 12.92 | 15.69 | 23.07 | 21.20 | 2.26 | 7.49 | 16.05 |
| 1997 | 34.40 | 16.27 | 31.70 | 33.37 | 30.28 | (25.11) | (4.37) | 20.41 |
| 1998 | (7.03) | 0.38 | 14.93 | 28.58 | 33.61 | 8.04 | 15.46 | 13.63 |
| 1999 | 10.76 | 47.73 | 1.89 | 21.03 | 28.16 | 20.15 | 32.87 | 22.83 |
| 2000 | 1.03 | (18.42) | 8.20 | (9.10) | (13.53) | (5.69) | (16.08) | (7.27) |
| 2001 | 35.43 | 6.00 | (0.47) | (11.88) | (15.17) | (10.69) | (22.03) | (1.05) |
| 2002 | (10.20) | (28.07) | (27.71) | (22.11) | (21.95) | 1.78 | (13.76) | (18.80) |
| Annualized Returns % | 15.42 | 9.19 | 13.04 | 10.81 | 9.50 | 14.88 | 12.28 | 12.72 |
| Standard Returns % | 20.96 | 25.67 | 17.59 | 17.52 | 19.29 | 30.19 | 26.57 | 17.72 |
| Years Best | 8 | 3 | 5 | 1 | 4 | 8 | 4 | 0 |
| Years Worst | 2 | 9 | 4 | 1 | 6 | 7 | 4 | 0 |

*Diversified Portfolio = 16% in each U.S. Asset Class, 10% in each International Asset Class. Source: *Returns Program,* Dimensional Fund Advisors (Rogers Capital Management, Inc.)

**Past performance is not an indicator of future expected returns.**

earnings is good—everything is going great—they are just small. Because they are doing so well, they don't have to pay as much for capital as other companies.

**THE THIRD COLUMN: Large-value stocks** — From the largest 90 percent of market universe[3], these *have the highest BtM ratios.* They are large companies that are distressed, because they are not doing so well.

**THE FOURTH COLUMN: S&P 500 (Standard & Poors 500)** — An index of stocks composed of the 500 largest companies in the U.S. The index is market weighted, which means the larger the company, the larger the weight in the index. The index is widely used as a stock benchmark for account performance measurement. This index includes 400 industrial stocks, 20 transportation stocks, 40 financial stocks, and 40 public utilities whether growth, value or those stocks in between.

**THE FIFTH COLUMN: Large-growth stocks** — Largest 90 percent of market universe* with the lowest BtMs in the top 10th percentile are chosen. These companies are doing very well, and they just happen to be very big also.

**THE SIXTH COLUMN: International large stocks** — The largest 60-75 percent by market cap ranking in Australia, Austria, Belgium, Denmark, Sweden, Finland, France, Germany, Greece, Hong Kong, Ireland, Italy, Japan, the Netherlands, New Zealand, Norway, Portugal, Singapore, Spain, Switzerland, and the UK.

**THE SEVENTH COLUMN: International small stocks** — The smallest 8 percent of companies in the following regions: Japan, UK, Austria, Belgium, Denmark, Finland, France, Germany, Greece, Ireland, Italy, the Netherlands, Norway, Spain, Sweden, Switzerland, Australia, Hong Kong, New Zealand, and Singapore.

**THE EIGHTH COLUMN: A diversified portfolio made up of all asset classes.** We wanted this diversified portfolio to be structured without bias, so it is a ratio of 80 percent U.S. stocks and 20 percent international. We divided 80 by five, which gave us 16

---

[3] Market Universe is defined as all stocks in the NYSE, AMEX, and NASDAQ. Source: Dimensional Fund Advisors Firm Profile & Returns Program.

percent in each of the five U.S. asset classes; and put 10 percent in each of the international asset classes. This portfolio is for the person who says, "Since I don't know what to do, I'll just divide my money equally among the asset classes."

## The Sun Does Not Shine on the Same Dog's Tail Every Day

The light gray boxes ▢ depict the worst performing asset class for that year. The dark gray boxes ▢ depict the best performing asset class for that year. The black boxes ▮ represent years when the diversified portfolio outperformed the S&P 500.

Do you see any pattern in the chart? Does it appear that one asset class is superior? No, if you look closely, it's totally random. The people who are trying to time the dark and light gray chart will always fail miserably. (Dalbar studies support this claim.)

The down years of '73 and '74 are intentionally included in the chart. Look at the best asset classes during those years. If we'd started the chart in '75, overall returns would have been a lot higher.

Now cover up the top row containing the names of the asset classes. Look at the data near the bottom of the chart, showing the annualized return, standard deviation and the number of years that the asset class was best or worst. If you had only this information and you could invest in just one asset class, which would you pick? You would most likely choose small value because of its annualized return of 15.42 percent.

Next, look at the year 1998. You'll see that small value returned a negative 7.03 percent, while large growth for that year was up 33.61 percent. That's a 40 percent difference. If someone had advised you 1998 to invest in the "best" asset class of small value, you would have underperformed by 40 percent. And you probably would have sold out after it did so poorly, especially because the financial media was telling people that value would never be good again.

But in 2001, the chart shows that small value was up 35.43 percent and large growth did a negative 15 percent, a 50 percent difference. What this tells you is not to invest all of your money in any one asset class. The sea of light and dark areas in this chart shows that every asset class behaves differently and without predictability at any given time. This is why all of them are necessary to build a successful portfolio.

Let's compare small growth and small value over the 33-year period from 1970 through 2002. Small value outperforms small growth. During that same period, large value outperforms large growth. Why did value outperform growth? Value companies are the poorest companies and are therefore riskier. Their cost of capital is greater. It's the same principle that the person who can least afford the loan pays the highest interest rates. During the years '95 to '98, there were hundreds of media articles proclaiming that value was dead. But look at 1995 on the chart—large value was up 38 percent.

On the other hand, large growth companies, such as GE or Microsoft, are highly successful companies, but look at their returns. If asset classes all paid the same rate of return, we would all buy large growth because it's the safest. Small outperforms large because large is safer.

> If asset classes all paid the same rate of return, we would all buy large growth because it's the safest. Small outperforms large because large is safer.

Academic studies have shown that international investing is no different when it comes to the risk factors—international value beats international growth; international small value beats international small growth. In other words, small has always beaten large over long periods of time. This is exactly the same for value verses growth.

Over 2,057 stocks make up the small-value asset class. You could buy any one of the small-value stocks and it might or might not perform like the asset class, but if you bought them all, you would get the return indicated. There is safety in numbers.

So how do you find out the asset class of the mutual funds you're invested in?

You can look up your fund on Morningstar.com or work with a knowledgeable investment advisor. They break everything down into asset classes for you.

Refer to the last large box on the chart labeled "Standard Deviation." The number in the box under each asset class represents the volatility of the asset class. The higher the number, the greater the volatility or (risk). While it was generally accepted that the large-growth asset class is safest, notice that the Standard Deviation for large growth is somewhat higher than the large value or the S&P 500 asset class. However, it is lower than either International asset class and either U.S. small-asset class.

> **By combining asset classes that have individually high Standard Deviation (volatility/risk), you are able to diversify away the higher risk inherent with any one asset class and achieve a superior return when compared to the "safest" asset class.**

Why is this significant? Because it demonstrates the overlooked power of diversification. Notice that a diversified portfolio provides a 3% higher annualized compound return than Large Growth over the 33-year period; yet it had 1½ % less volatility. By combining asset classes that have individually high Standard Deviation (volatility/risk), you are able to diversify away the higher risk inherent with any one asset class and achieve a superior return when compared to the "safest" asset class.

Many 401(k)s have no small funds and no international funds; but, it is impossible to build a portfolio without a representation of each asset class. If you don't have all the asset classes in your 401(k), then you need to insist that you have at least a representative fund in every asset class. That's one of your rights.

Let's say your 401(k) includes Vanguard Growth Index and the Oakmark Fund. You should have an S&P 500 index, but you would want to use all three of those to fill up the rows across the top of the chart. The S&P 500 is a blend of value and growth. You may want to add Vanguard Fund for large growth and Oakmark Fund for large value. You have to at least have large growth and value and small growth and value. Forget the mid-caps if you have to, but you have to have international to some degree. You need a pure international, not a worldwide fund such as Janus Worldwide (80 percent of Janus Worldwide was in U.S. to attempt to boost their return). If you don't have international growth and international value, it's going to be hard to build a truly diversified portfolio.

## Summary

- Asset class refers to a *category* of investments.
- There are nine asset-class categories.
- Asset-class performance is totally random.
- You can combine asset classes in a portfolio to lower risk.

Diversification is just one of the six investment principles that will give you the highest possible probability for success. Learn what all six are and how to put them to work for you in the next chapter.

# Chapter 6

## LEARN THE SIX
## PRINCIPLES OF
## SUCCESSFUL INVESTING

### Investing Is a Marathon, Not a Sprint!

Twenty-five years ago, before the "technology boom," the greatest technology company in the world was IBM. IBM dominated the market; no other company was even close. Logically, that should have been the best investment, but others were better. For example, Clorox Corporation, a bleach company, outperformed IBM.

Why can't people who are highly educated in the world of finance pick a superior stock or fund? Because they don't have a crystal ball, and no one knows what will happen in the future. But the good news is that it isn't necessary.

We know how to *blend* the markets to mitigate risk. There are six principles you can employ to put together the hand you've been dealt in a way that gives you a chance to smooth out market volatility and give you the highest possible probability for success. These principles work together to level out the roller-coaster ride associated with good and bad markets and produce steady results.

1. **Dollar Cost Averaging**
2. **Diversification**
3. **Asset Allocation**
4. **Asset-Class Investing**
5. **Time**
6. **Rebalancing**

The best reason I can give you for learning how to use these basic principles of successful investing is to lessen your *fear factor*. You will no longer have to play the role of the blind sheep, just following someone else's lead because you're unable to make informed decisions. Nor do you have to get a Ph.D. in finance; simple knowledge is your best protection. Once you have a grasp of how these concepts work, you can take an active role in putting them to work in your favor.

## Principle One — Dollar Cost Averaging

Dollar cost averaging is a systematic purchasing of shares with fixed dollar amounts at regular intervals, without regard to the share price. It has many advantages and very few drawbacks, if any.

It works like this: A 401(k) participant decides he/she is going to defer $100 of his/her paycheck every pay period, which is semi-monthly. So twice each month the participant automatically buys $100 worth of shares, purchasing more shares when the price is down, and fewer when the price is up. It has been academically proven that this method will lower your average cost-per-share over time.

Example: We decide to invest $100 per/month to buy longhorn cattle. In January, the price of longhorn cattle is $10 per head, so a hundred dollars buys 10 head. By February, the price of longhorn cattle

### Figure 6.1   DOLLAR COST AVERAGING
#### Longhorns and Dollar Cost Averaging

Monthly Commitment. . . . . . . . . . . . . . .$100.00 to Longhorn Cattle

| | | | |
|---|---|---|---|
| January | $100.00/$10.00 | equals | 10 Cattle |
| February | $100.00/$ 5.00 | equals | 20 Cattle |
| March | $100.00/$ 2.50 | equals | 40 Cattle |
| April | $100.00/$ 5.00 | equals | 20 Cattle |
| May | $100.00/$10.00 | equals | 10 Cattle |
| Total of: $500.00 | | spent to purchase: 100 Cattle | |

**$1,000** Sales proceeds yield profit of $500.00 on a **non-appreciating** asset.

has dropped 50 percent to $5 per head. That means the original investment is worth only half as much, but a hundred dollars now buys 20 head. The next month, the price has dropped again and the original investment is down 75 percent, but now we can buy 40 head with our $100. The price starts to rebound in April to $5 a head, so we buy another 20 head. Finally, in May, the price of longhorn cattle is back to the original purchase price at $10 per head and we buy 10 head. At this point, we decide to get out of the cattle business. Let's do our accounting. We spent $500 and bought 100 head of cattle. At the end of May, cattle are selling

> **Dollar cost averaging is a systematic purchasing of shares with fixed dollar amounts at regular intervals, without regard to the share price. It has many advantages and very few drawbacks, if any.**

for our original purchase price of $10 per head, so our 100 head brings $1000 gross. After deducting the $500 we spent to acquire the cattle, we actually made $500 on an asset that never appreciated above the original purchase price!

Dollar cost averaging keeps investors from making some critical mistakes, such as market timing, and trading themselves into oblivion. Here are examples of the two most common investing errors:

**1** **INVESTOR A** has a diversified portfolio, but can't control his emotional reactions. He receives a quarterly statement in which three of his funds show a modest gain and two funds each show a 15 percent loss, resulting in a portfolio total that is down for that period. At this point, most "long-term" investors become quarterly investors, meaning they are overwhelmed with an urge to "fix" their portfolios by putting new money only toward the funds that made money and dumping the two that lost money.

Does this make sense? Of course not, because it means the investor is "buying high and selling low." Everyone, regardless of their investment experience, knows how important it is to do the opposite: "buy low and sell high." Yet, it's the hardest of all principles for investors, without guidance, to follow! It's not in our nature to buy funds that are struggling, and is in our nature to join the bandwagon of the latest winner.

Almost without fail, Investor A will dump his mutual funds that have lost money and take the 15 percent loss (which before selling, was only an *un*realized loss). Then, to make matters worse, Investor A buys more of the "best" fund, which happens to be the highest priced. Now the funds switch and the two that have lost money begin to rebound and the recent winners start to lag. And the losing cycle is born.

**2** **INVESTOR B** suffers from market timing. Although he also has a diversified portfolio and is able to overcome his urge to sell his securities when they are down, Investor B instead decides to sit on the sidelines during bad markets. In other words, he thinks it is wiser to stop contributing altogether during bear markets, and will come back when the market is "good" again. Essentially, this investor has acknowledged that the market will turn around again.

So why not buy shares at cheap prices when the market is down, if you think it will eventually go back up? In fact, it's the best time to buy, and definitely not the time to stop your contributions to your 401(k). Additionally, if the employer provides a match, then free money is being left on the table. That's like walking past a $100 bill and being too lazy to bend over and pick it up.

In both of the above cases, the discipline of dollar cost averaging takes the worry and guesswork out of investing and is a more methodical and sensible way to invest. By setting up dollar cost averaging contributions in a diversified portfolio, you'll always own some things that perform better than others. However, by making regular deposits and purchasing more shares on a consistent basis, you're not as worried about which ones are up or down. In fact, you can take comfort in knowing that you are purchasing more shares with your contribution when certain funds may be down; and when the fund turns around, the investor with the most shares will be in the best shape!

**If you decide to sit on the sidelines and not continue to invest, the rest of these principles won't matter.**

# Principle Two — Diversification

*The biggest mistake most participants make is attempting to diversify within the same asset class.*

Diversification may well be the most misused word in the English language. Participants frequently say, "I'm well diversified; I have four funds." But, they're not really diversified because their four funds are all in the same asset class — large growth funds for instance. Suppose your plan has many choices, but they're all in the same asset class. How could this happen? Your 401(k) provider probably picked them based on best performance, which would have come from the same asset class. So he ended up with three large-cap funds, thinking he was making the plan diversified. This is why you have to know what you're doing, or at least have an advisor who does.

Harry Markowitz, a Nobel Prize winner in economics, said while almost all diversification is good, there is *effective* diversification and *ineffective* diversification. Simply put, if your investments move up and down together, that is ineffective diversification and has the same effect as being invested in just one fund. Chances are, there is also a tremendous stock overlap in these funds.

> **A truly diversified portfolio is comprised of many asset classes, some of which are doing well, and some of which are not doing so well.**

A diversified portfolio provides stability and, hence, a larger long-term return; but only if you spread your money among the various asset classes that don't always have the same price movements — for example, between value and growth; small and large; international growth and value. A truly diversified portfolio is comprised of many asset classes, some of which are doing well, and some of which are not doing so well. Thus, the total return of a diversified portfolio will never be as good as the current best asset class; nor will it ever be as poor as the worst. **But the ride will be smoother and the end result will be a superior return.**

> **Asset allocation simply means determining what proportion of your money is going to be invested in which asset classes — stocks, bonds, and cash investments — in order to maximize the growth of your portfolio for each unit of risk that you take.**

# Principle Three — Asset Allocation

Asset allocation simply means determining what proportion of your money is going to be invested in which asset classes — stocks, bonds, and cash investments — in order to maximize the growth of your portfolio for each unit of risk that you take. This may be the single most important determinant of the long-term performance of any investment portfolio. The confusion occurs when the terms "asset allocation" and "diversification" are used interchangeably. Even if you are 100 percent invested in money-market funds, that is still a form of asset allocation.

The first step is to identify what asset classes are represented by the mutual funds in your plan and then spread, or allocate, your contributions among them to minimize risk.

You should insist on a mutual fund that represents every asset class we just discussed. You may discover that your employer has given you only cash, a bond fund and four large growth funds. That's not asset allocation.

### Now, how do you determine what percentage of each asset class you should own?

Selecting asset classes with a low correlation to each other is the Nobel Prize-winning secret for achieving more consistent portfolio performance. Academics have actually calculated methods to measure correlation in a portfolio, thereby enabling the volatility or risk of a portfolio to be measured with greater degrees of predictability.

Because of these measurement tools, it is possible to combine in a portfolio assets that have the potential to generate higher returns due to their volatile nature, but whose market performances have a low correlation to one another. This achieves the result that the portfolio as a whole will actually be less risky than any one of the individual investments, yet generate a higher overall return than a portfolio made up solely of low-risk investments. The longest time period of data available will provide the most accurate correlation.

## Principle Four — Asset-Class Investing

Asset-class investing is easy to understand: first, determine what proportion of your money is going to be invested in which asset classes, select your allocation, and then leave it alone!

Asset-class funds are *passively* managed, which means there is **no** "active" decision-making occurring about buying and selling the issues that are contained within the mutual fund. Their sole purpose is to mimic the markets while experiencing very low turnover, and significantly below average costs.

The best way to do asset-class investing is by owning asset-class mutual funds or institutional asset-class mutual funds because they are more reliable in concentrating on a specific asset class. These funds are a relatively new hybrid, created by institutional money managers — such as Dimensional Fund Advisors. Although not available to the general public, institutional asset-class mutual funds can be purchased by participants through selected groups of investment advisors who are required to educate their clients on the benefits of passive asset-class investing.

> **Asset-class investing is easy to understand: first, determine what proportion of your money is going to be invested in which asset classes, select your allocation, and then leave it alone!**

If asset-class mutual funds are available in your plan, they are worth your consideration. If not, go to the next principle.

Some of the more progressive 401(k) plans have predefined asset-class *portfolios* representing various levels of risk; these portfolios vary only by the percent allotted to bonds. For example, a conservative portfolio may have 40 percent stock mutual funds and 60 percent bond mutual funds, while an aggressive may have 80 percent stock and 20 percent bond funds.

> **It is very difficult to maintain a balanced portfolio with actively managed funds because of *style drift*.**

Actively managed mutual funds (especially the advertised ones that appeal to the retail market) tend to do what we call *style drift*. Active managers are under tremendous pressure to deliver returns, even though that may not be the function of a particular fund. They will drift out of their asset class into another asset class in an effort to, hopefully, boost their returns.

It is very difficult to maintain a balanced portfolio with actively managed funds because of style drift. Let's say you wanted a portfolio that is a 50-50 mix of large-growth companies and small-value companies. If the manager of the fund of large-growth companies starts buying small-value companies because large growth isn't doing well, or vice versa, that messes up your 50-50 allocation.

And, if every fund went to large growth when growth is doing well, then when growth plummeted, your whole portfolio would plummet. That's why many investors today are down 70 percent. They may have tried to remain diversified, but the managers of those funds drifted. If each one "fudged" just a little in the direction of whatever was up at the time, it would be enough to cause big trouble to a portfolio. Your employer or his representative should search for managers that have been consistent and that will not chase returns in a neighboring asset class to prop up returns.

They should monitor the managers, and if they start drifting, they should be replaced. This is the employer's fiduciary obligation.

It's a difficult concept to get across. Most 401(k) plans are simply sold a list of mutual funds from which participants may choose. This is to avoid any liability if something goes wrong. Participants, without any knowledge or advice, naturally pick the funds with the best returns for the last period, and that's how they end up with everything in one asset class.

Then, if the fund doesn't deliver performance, investors take their money out of that mutual fund and go elsewhere. And the fund manager gets fired. The average tenure of an active manager is around three years. Robert Sanborn is one of the top value-fund managers who got fired for *sticking* with value companies when growth was in vogue. He was later exonerated because, after a few years, value was again back in vogue.

Asset-class funds and index funds are not under pressure to perform like actively managed funds. If asset-class funds are not available, the next best alternative is to build a portfolio of index funds. Even though they are only numerical commercial benchmarks, and not academically defined, as asset-class funds are, it is still possible to build a superior portfolio with index funds. For example, the S&P 500 is a good one to utilize; and frankly, the large-growth managers have trouble beating it. Each year, the S&P 500 index outperforms 82 to 95 percent of the actively managed funds whose stated goal is to beat the S&P 500.

## Principle Five — Time

The longer the time period you hold your investments, the closer you will come to the expected average. This means short-term market fluctuations gets smoothed out over time.

No serious investor would knowingly hold a stock for only one day, one month, or even one year. Such brief time periods are clearly too short for investment in stocks, because the expected variation in returns is too large in comparison with the average expected return. Such short-term holdings in stocks are not investments; they are *speculations*.

Equities become much less volatile the longer they're held. Bonds and money-market funds are lower risk, lower return, and can be held a shorter time.

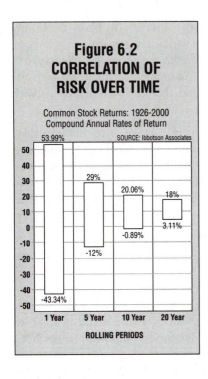

**Figure 6.2**
## CORRELATION OF RISK OVER TIME

Common Stock Returns: 1926-2000
Compound Annual Rates of Return

53.99%     SOURCE: Ibbotson Associates

29%
20.06%
18%
-0.89%
3.11%
-12%
-43.34%

1 Year   5 Year   10 Year   20 Year

**ROLLING PERIODS**

If you study Figure 6.2, you will see that the common stock investments made in any one-year period could have gone up 54 percent or dropped 43 percent. But, when you look at any 20-year period, you will see that there are no down years—only gains.

If we measure an investment every three years, rather than every quarter, we can see satisfying progress that wouldn't be apparent in a quarterly measurement. In most cases, the time horizon that investors use as the standard to measure results is far too short, causing dissatisfaction with investment performance.

### The Power of Compounding is just a function of time.

Compounding is the process of earning a rate of return on your money that is invested, and then reinvesting those earnings at the same rate. This can be done with dividends, interest or new contributions. For example, a $100 investment, earning compound interest, at 10 percent a year, would accumulate to $110 at the end of the first year, and $121 at the end of the second year, and so on. The actual formula is: compound sum = (principal) (1 + interest rate) to the nth_power, where n is the number of years.

The essence of the formula is that at the end of each year, interest is earned not only on the original amount, but also on all the previously accumulated interest amounts—you are earning interest on interest!

The typical compounding table (Figure 6.3) shows you how a single investment of $10,000 will grow at various rates of return. Five percent is what you might get from a Certificate of Deposit (CD), or with a government bond; 10 percent is about the historical average stock market return, and 16 percent would have been possible over the last twenty years: but historically, you should average around 11 percent.

| | **Figure 6.3** VARIOUS GROWING RATES | | |
|---|---|---|---|
| Year | 5% | 10% | 15% |
| | $10,000 | $ 10,000 | $ 10,000 |
| 5 | $12,800 | $ 16,100 | $ 20,100 |
| 10 | $16,300 | $ 25,900 | $ 40,500 |
| 15 | $20,800 | $ 41,800 | $ 81,400 |
| 25 | $33,900 | $108,300 | $329,200 |

A simple way to figure how long it takes your money to double is the *Rule of 72*. Divide the number 72 by the interest rate or rate of return you are earning and the result is the number of years it takes your money to double. For example, if you are earning 10 percent, your money will double in 7.2 years. If you are earning 12 percent, it only takes six years for your money to double.

Your goal is to maximize the rate of return you are earning, and to minimize the risk you are taking. If you can earn just 10 percent in twenty years, because of compounding, your money will have grown by almost 800 percent.

## Principle Six — Rebalancing

The principle of rebalancing is to maintain the same percentages in the various asset classes you have chosen, to maintain proper diversification in all market environments. By rebalancing, you may give up some short-term gains if you reduce your holdings of winning stocks prematurely, but you'll also miss the big losses when and if they collapse.

Many investment advisors rebalanced their equity positions down to their allocation targets as the bull market pushed equity values upward. In 2002 they increased equity positions as the declining markets dropped those positions below targets. As a result, they have been selling high, then buying low. See the logic?

When the price is down, you are able to buy more shares. Plus, you're reinvesting the money you've made along with your principal and *compounding* your growth.

More frequent rebalancing improves results, which would indicate that a style that is outperforming the broad market does not stay in favor for long periods of time. The same holds true for a style that is underperforming the broad market: its out-of-favor status does not sustain for long periods of time.

Rebalancing an investment portfolio seems simple on the surface, but as you start to think through the method, frequency, tolerance limits, fees, and commissions, the subject reveals itself to be quite complex and without easy answers. This is probably not an exercise that an average 401(k) investor would pursue on his or her own. Here's where a qualified advisor can help. Although with more progressive plans, you can go to your computer, push a button and it will automatically rebalance your 401(k) portfolio.

An investment advisor or consultant should be knowledgeable about the various issues surrounding rebalancing, and, ideally, should be able to explain them to you in a way that makes the desired method acceptable and practical to apply.

## Summary

- **Dollar Cost Averaging**
- **Diversification**
- **Asset Allocation**
- **Asset-Class Investing**
- **Time**
- **Rebalancing**

These principles work together to level out the roller-coaster ride associated with good and bad markets, and produce steady results.

But, you still need to understand your investment choices — the subject of the next Building Block.

*Chapter 7*

# LEARN TO UNDERSTAND YOUR INVESTMENT CHOICES

Knowing what your investment choices are and understanding how they affect the outcome of your retirement income are two entirely different things.

When you receive your enrollment form worksheet, you will be asked to fill in what percentage of your salary you want to contribute. Usually just below that is a list of funds offered. A typical plan offers, on average, six to eight funds covering the available choices — a money-market fund, a bond fund, three or four U.S. equity funds, and an international fund. You must indicate how you want your contribution to be invested, by percentage(s), to which of the funds being offered. You can generally pick as few or as many as you want. This will depend on your chosen investment strategy. If the funds offered are not sufficient to build a diversified portfolio, you should insist on having whatever is missing added to your plan.

It is your responsibility to wade through any prospectus included in your enrollment kit. Under current SEC rules, a prospectus (a comprehensive legal document explaining everything you could possibly want to know about the mutual fund) must be provided on your request and in most cases is provided automatically if you invest in a particular mutual fund.

However, a prospectus is very difficult reading and most participants get no real benefit from attempting to understand it. What is needed is information provided in a simple, direct format. The good news is that the SEC is recommending new rules, including requiring the translation of the fund booklets into easily understood language, and the creation of a clearly written one-page summary — a streamlined profile that includes a mutual fund's vital statistics. Such documents must be updated at least once a year.

To get easy-to-understand and up-to-date information on the fees, objectives, performance and which asset class this fund belongs to, you may go to a website that provides this information (such as Morningstar.com). If your 401(k) plan has a website, this information may be provided there. Since a high percentage of 401(k) plan participants fall into the category of "uninformed investors," it is in the plan sponsors' best interest to provide as much education as possible about the funds offered.

## Investment Vehicle Choices

ERISA 404(c) says you must have at least three investment options with different risk and return characteristics. You might have a money market, a bond fund and a stock fund or an international fund, but typically plans have six to eight choices. Too many choices may confuse participants; too few may not allow for a successful retirement strategy. (*See* Figure 7.1)

> **ERISA 404(c) says you must have at least three investment options with different risk and return characteristics.**

The following descriptions are very broad but provide a beginning guideline of what you are looking at if they appear as investment choices in your plan.

## Types of Mutual Funds

Think of a mutual fund as a financial intermediary that pools all its investors' funds together and buys stocks, bonds, and/or other assets on behalf of the group as a whole. Each investor (your 401(k) plan) receives a regular statement indicating the value of its own

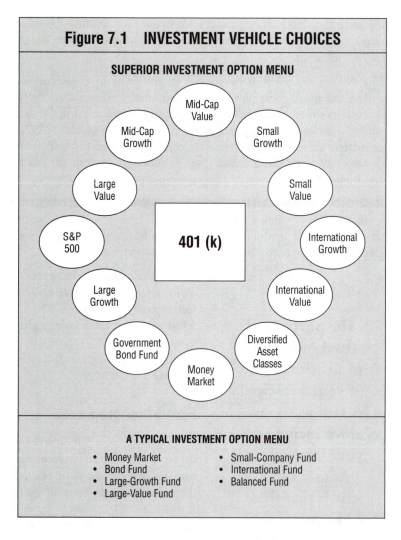

**Figure 7.1   INVESTMENT VEHICLE CHOICES**

SUPERIOR INVESTMENT OPTION MENU

Mid-Cap Value

Mid-Cap Growth

Small Growth

Large Value

Small Value

S&P 500

**401 (k)**

International Growth

Large Growth

International Value

Government Bond Fund

Diversified Asset Classes

Money Market

**A TYPICAL INVESTMENT OPTION MENU**

- Money Market
- Bond Fund
- Large-Growth Fund
- Large-Value Fund

- Small-Company Fund
- International Fund
- Balanced Fund

shares within the total investment pool. Your particular shares are accounted for daily by the plan administrator.

Mutual funds continually issue new shares of the fund for sale to the public, and every new purchase results in new shares being issued. The number of shares and the price are directly related to the value of the securities the mutual fund holds. A fund's share price can change from day to day, depending on the daily value of its underlying securities. Each share's value is computed by dividing the total value of all the assets held by the fund by the number of shares issued and outstanding.

The NAV reflects the daily change in the price of the securities within the fund's portfolio, and is computed at the end of every day that the markets are open for trading. In a regular mutual fund, which includes thousands and often millions of shares, the NAV is calculated on a daily basis without commissions, in full and fractional units, with values moving up or down along with the stock and bond markets.

**Reference Only:** Special Brokerage Accounts or individually directed accounts allow participants to buy and sell in any mutual fund or security available in the retail market. While this sounds great and glamorous, these accounts have had the lowest returns.

> The purpose of fixed income is to provide safety of your principal as well as to produce income on your investment. Another benefit is that fixed income of the right type can dampen (reduce) the volatility of your investment portfolio.

These plans charge the participants a fee for this service. The fees typically range from $50 to $300 a year for the account, plus transaction charges ranging up to $30, not including commissions on stock transactions.

## Fixed-Income Funds

Most fixed-income funds will be called bond funds because the primary investment is in bonds, the most common form of debt instrument. Other debt instruments include government and corporate issues. The purpose of fixed income is to provide safety of your principal as well as to produce income on your investment. Another benefit is that fixed income of the right type can dampen (reduce) the volatility of your investment portfolio.

The main risks associated with bond funds are: market, or price, risk if interest rates rise; and credit risk if the ability of the borrowers to repay the debt declines. The longer the maturity of the bonds in the fund, the more susceptible the fund is to price risk if interest rates rise. For example, a fund with 2-year average maturities on its bonds will not suffer a decline in value nearly as much as a fund in which the bonds average 8-10 year maturities.

For safety, look for U.S. Government bond funds or at least a Corporate Bond Fund that invests in bonds that are AA to AAA quality.

## Classes of Fixed Income Funds

### MONEY-MARKET FUNDS

Money-market funds are the safest type of mutual funds if you are worried about the risk of losing your principal. Money-market funds are like bank savings accounts, in that the value of your investment does not fluctuate. Money-market funds, however, are not insured like bank certificates of deposit. The interest rates are generally lower than other forms of fixed-income funds.

### GOVERNMENT BOND FUNDS

These funds invest in debt from the U.S. government. They are by their nature quite conservative, depending upon the maturity of the underlying bonds. They generally invest in all types of government bonds, including those backed by the government but not directly issued by the government. Look for bond maturities of 5 years or less.

### U.S. FIXED INCOME

These are funds that invest in all types of U.S. bonds, including government and corporate bonds. They will typically invest in higher-quality investments with little risk of default across a broad range of maturities. Check to see that the credit quality of the bonds is primarily AAA or AA and the average maturities are no longer than 5 years.

### HIGH YIELD FUNDS (Junk Bonds)

These funds typically invest in low-quality corporate debt and are subject to high risk of default. They, therefore, tend to offer a higher yield. If safety and stability are important to you, avoid this choice. For similar risk, you could have higher potential returns in equity mutual funds.

## GLOBAL BOND FUNDS

These funds invest in foreign and U.S. bonds. Historically, global bond funds have outperformed domestic bond funds, but you do assume some additional risk.

## INTERNATIONAL BOND FUNDS

These funds specialize in investing in bonds of foreign governments and companies and are usually riskier than U.S. investments. However, you may realize additional income as compared to U.S. Fixed Income.

# Equity Funds

A stock mutual fund is called an equity fund, which is usually a higher-growth vehicle. Over the last 15 years, the average stock mutual fund has returned about 11.3 percent on an annual basis. But remember the rule: the greater the return, the greater the risk and volatility. Obviously, an equity mutual fund, because of its investment risk, is not an appropriate investment for your short-term money or for your intermediate money. But, if the time frame for your long-term money is 8-10 years or more, an equity mutual fund is a good choice.

## Classes of Equity Funds

### GROWTH MUTUAL FUNDS

A growth company is one that is doing very well, by any measurement. A growth mutual fund is typically defined as one that invests in companies that are exceeding the growth of the economy. Investors look for companies and industries with a strong growth trend in sales and earnings. Growth companies typically sell at high price/ earnings (P/E) ratios, reflecting the expectation that their growth will continue and that the earnings will eventually "catch up" with the high valuations awarded the companies. Growth companies and growth mutual funds can cover all capitalization ranges.

- **Large-Cap Growth**
  An investment strategy that invests in stocks of large high-growth companies with a capitalization of approximately $10 billion or greater.

- **Mid-Cap Growth**

  An investment strategy that invests in stocks of mid-sized companies with a capitalization of between $2 billion and $10 billion.

- **Small-Cap Growth**

  An investment strategy that invests in stocks of smaller companies with a capitalization of less than $2 billion.

## VALUE MUTUAL FUNDS

Value mutual funds invest in companies that are distressed. Value stocks have high book-to-market ratios, which means the stock is trading at a low price compared with its book value. (Book value is defined as the company's assets on a balance sheet, less its liabilities, and is often figured on a per/share basis.) In addition, the price/earnings ratio is lower for value stocks, and as such, are generally considered to be less volatile. As with growth stocks, value stocks can cover all capitalization ranges.

> **A stock mutual fund is called an equity fund, which is usually a higher-growth vehicle. Over the last 15 years, the average stock mutual fund has returned about 11.3 percent on an annual basis. But remember the rule: the greater the return, the greater the risk and volatility.**

- **Large-Cap Value**

  An investment strategy that invests in stocks of large companies with a capitalization of approximately $10 billion or greater.

- **Mid-Cap Value**

  An investment strategy that invests in stocks of mid-sized companies with a capitalization of between $2 billion and $10 billion.

- **Small-Cap Value**

  An investment strategy that invests in stocks of smaller companies with a capitalization of less than $2 billion.

> **While value stocks have outperformed growth stocks over long periods of time, it is important to have both in your portfolio to stabilize returns.**

Value and growth stocks tend to behave differently. There are market cycles when value stocks outperform growth stocks, and other periods when growth stocks outperform value stocks. In general, a growth investor's returns are somewhat more volatile than a value investor's returns. Both styles in a portfolio can even out performance over time. When one group is underperforming the market, the other is outperforming it. While value stocks have outperformed growth stocks over long periods of time, it is important to have both in your portfolio to stabilize returns.

## International Equities Funds

The principles of international growth and value are the same as domestic. Growth companies are those that are doing very well. Value companies are those that are distressed and doing poorly by almost any measurement.

### INTERNATIONAL GROWTH
These funds focus on a portfolio of stocks of high-growth international companies.

### INTERNATIONAL VALUE
These funds focus on a portfolio of stocks of distressed companies worldwide.

## Summary

- Insist on education on the fund choices in your 401(k).
- Insist on any missing funds necessary to create your diversified portfolio.

- Mutual funds are the most prevalent of the investment vehicles selected and are the building blocks for your investment portfolio.

Just as important as selecting the right investments is building an appropriate core investment *strategy* that the investor can adhere to that delivers a consistent and specific result. Our next Building Block will show you how.

# Chapter 8

## LEARN HOW TO DESIGN A WELL-BALANCED INVESTMENT PORTFOLIO

A t a time when 40l(k) plan participants can have greater control over their assets than ever before, it's a sad fact, but few participants are even aware that they can make investment allocations, or otherwise direct how their plan contributions are invested. Or, if they are vaguely aware of their rights, they don't know how or where to begin.

Many participants in 401(k) plans have no other investing experience. Few have ever read the academic research of investing, some of which has won the Nobel Prize. What little information they do have comes from television, newspapers and magazines, or co-worker conversations. Most of this "noise" is misguided, sensationalized, and lacks any foundation. Many false ideas are so widespread that the public, for the most part, simply accepts them as fact.

Often, plan contribution election forms are presented to the new employee along with insurance documents, confidentiality agreements, etc., upon hiring—all to be completed and returned the next day. Intimidating legal jargon and overriding priorities of the moment may force a selection of anything familiar, usually whatever low-risk, fixed-income vehicle is available. After all, this is retirement money we're talking about here! But, in truth, that's exactly why you want to take an active role in directing the investments that will become a contributing factor in the comfort level you will enjoy later in life.

Even if you need to make a decision immediately, most plans allow the participant the freedom to transfer between investment options on a daily basis. That's not to suggest that you should abuse this freedom by chasing the latest "hot picks" or attempting to time the market. Both are strategies that are costly to implement, have an extremely low probability of success, and are ineffective in adding value. Rather, it's to point out your ability to rebalance, or correct your choices, as you become more informed.

To make informed choices, arm yourself with the basic terminology and strategies in this book and get the specific rules of your 401(k) plan. Ask your plan representative to contact financial consultants and set up investment education. They will be able to explain your various investment alternatives, as well as how the plan is monitored. Most 401(k) plans have a long-term, systematic manner of monitoring any investment progress. If you're going to direct your investments, you will need to know how you can receive periodic performance (gain and loss) results.

> **The only way to protect against investment losses, and still achieve a reasonable growth rate of return, is by creating a portfolio with an optimal combination of investments for a specific level of risk.**

## Protecting Your Investment

Some people think that the money in 401(k) plans is insured against any loss. It depends on what kind of loss you're talking about. Federal law requires that trustees be bonded by an insurance company, which reimburses the trust in the case of fraud, embezzlement, or other criminal activity. However, your money is *not* protected against *investment losses*. Contrary to some beliefs, the Federal government does not guarantee your account in any manner in defined-contribution plans such as a 401(k) plan. Your best protection is your investment knowledge. The only way to protect against investment losses, and still achieve a reasonable growth rate of return, is by creating a portfolio with an optimal combination of investments for a specific level of risk. The higher the expected growth of the investments, the higher the risk. The lower the risk, the lower the expected return. Real risk is not the volatility of periodic returns; rather, it is the probability of not having enough money to meet a financial goal, such as retirement.

## How Aggressive Do You Need to Be?

There are three factors that determine how aggressive you should be.

1. The amount of *gap* between the current rate of accumulation of your investments and your financial goals.

2. The amount of *time* you have before retirement. The more time you have to accumulate assets and recover from potential losses, the more aggressive your portfolio can be. Or, you can be more conservative if you will have more time to compound the earnings in lower-return investments.

3. Your fear factor. When do you jump ship and not follow your plan? Return to Building Block 4 and bring your risk tolerance percentage here.

If we ask participants how much they want to make, "As much as I can," they all say. Everybody thinks they'd love to be ultra aggressive. Who wants to make three percent per year? Everyone wants to make 15 percent, but most don't understand the amount of risk they may have to take to get it. This is where participants get into trouble. You have to think not in terms of how much you are willing to make, but how much you are willing to lose. That's the more important part of the equation. Determine a percentage of your assets that you can lose and still stick with the program.

## What Is a Reasonable Growth Rate of Return?

An informed investor needs to establish his or her personal expected *reasonable* growth rate of return. The general rule of thumb is that if you take the percentage of decline tolerance (how much money you could stand to lose) in a given quarter that you are comfortable with, divide that percentage in half, and add a money-market rate (typically 3 to 4 percent), the result is a reasonable rate of growth over a ten-year period.

Again, how little or how much risk you take directly affects how much growth you can expect. For instance, if you are willing to take a 10 percent decline quarterly, divide that number in half (5 percent), and add 3 to 4 percent. A reasonable rate of growth that you can expect to capture is 8 to 9 percent annually over a three- to five-year period.

It is important to know, *and remember,* that there will be some times when you will experience declines in excess of this amount and your returns might be superior at other times.

## How Do You Measure the Risk of an Investment?

You may have seen one of the old investment pyramid charts. They're in almost every basic investment book explaining risk and reward: safe investments such as cash at the bottom; bonds, stocks, and real estate in the middle; and more speculative investments at the top. Most 401(k) investors understand this hierarchy, but it's overly simplistic and not useful in designing portfolios.

In the financial industry, we use terms like *beta* and *volatility* and *standard deviation:*

- **Beta** is a measure of the risk of an investment, compared with that of the market. This is a good way for institutions to measure risk; however, it is often not very useful for you since we don't look at risk in relative terms (meaning in relation to something else). The market is said to have a beta of 1.0. If a mutual fund has a beta of 0.8, it is said to be 80 percent as risky as the market.

- **Volatility** is simply investment jargon for frequency and amount of change. Volatility is a measure of *total risk,* instead of *relative risk* like beta. It can be statistically measured using *standard deviation.*

- **Standard deviation** describes how far from the average performance the monthly performance has been, either higher or lower, and helps explain what the distribution of returns will likely be. The greater the range of returns, the greater the risk.

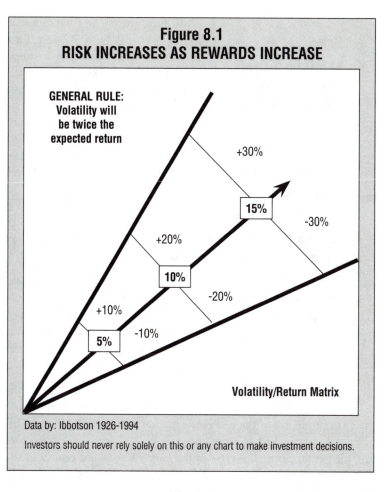

**Figure 8.1**
**RISK INCREASES AS REWARDS INCREASE**

GENERAL RULE:
Volatility will
be twice the
expected return

+30%

15%

-30%

+20%

10%

-20%

+10%

5%

-10%

**Volatility/Return Matrix**

Data by: Ibbotson 1926-1994

Investors should never rely solely on this or any chart to make investment decisions.

If you invest for a short-term goal, you will probably want lower volatility and be willing to accept lower returns. If you invest for the long-term, you can probably tolerate greater volatility in order to anticipate the potential for greater returns.

People are willing to accept risk when buying real estate because they don't purchase a house thinking that they might sell it tomorrow. They know that, despite occasional drops in the real-estate market, their house is probably going to increase in value by the time they've paid off the mortgage in 15 years or more. When you bought your house, you weren't thinking, "What are housing prices going to

> **Learn to expect the unexpected. What we want you to do is try to mentally prepare for market "corrections," commonly referred to as a bear market, when the stock market experiences a decline of more than 20 percent.**

do tomorrow?" You were investing over a 10- to 20-year time period, so you bought a home that met your needs and that you believed would increase in worth over the long term. Consider how you would feel about the risk of owning a home if you looked at the market prices every day: "The water main on Sixth Street broke; my house just dropped in value 10 percent." Odds are you wouldn't be a happy homeowner if you monitored your home's market value daily.

The same is true for stocks held over long periods. But for some reason people don't think about stocks the way they think about real estate. "Long term" is next quarter for most participants.

Different investments behave differently during different times. As an example, when the real-estate market was booming in the '70s, the stock market had some of its worst years. Large-cap stocks were the top performing asset class in the late '90s, but did poorly in the 2000, 2001 and 2002 years. Halfway through 2003, large-cap stocks (growth and value) were up substantially.

Learn to expect the unexpected. What we want you to do is try to mentally prepare for market "corrections," commonly referred to as a bear market, when the stock market experiences a decline of more than 20 percent. At times, the market has gone down and stayed down for a long time. At other times, it just dipped and flipped back up again.

The '90s were a time of sharp, quick drops and dramatic movements upward. This might have been because the inflow of information was much faster or it may have been just due to the economy. Our inflation rate was down, our political system was stable, and corporations were generating steady profits. All of these factors combined to create a bull market.

- Since WWII, there have been 42 years with positive market returns and only 11 years with negative returns.
- The best return was +45 percent in 1954.
- The worst was -29.7 percent in 1974.
- The median was +16.5 percent.
- The market has gone down two or more years in a row only twice, in 1973 and 1974, and again in 2000, 2001 and 2002.

The good times in the market have far outpaced the down periods, as you can see. When the economy is healthy and the market is on a roll, stock prices can rise for years. During the last 50 years, the stock market has seen four major bull markets, with moves over 100 percent; however, there were meaningful declines in between, even in those positive environments.

The main problems are that you don't have time to be checking on stocks or funds all during the day; and you don't have the expertise to trade in and out of the market during the up and down periods. (Don't feel badly — no one does.) The point of protecting your plan is also saving your time. Your time is better spent concentrating on your work.

> **If you have access to an advisor, work with him or her to develop a personal strategy in the form of a statement of investment objectives; then commit to it in writing and stick with it.**

If you have access to an advisor, work with him or her to develop a personal strategy in the form of a statement of investment objectives; then commit to it in writing and stick with it. Having your own personal investment plan for accumulating capital will

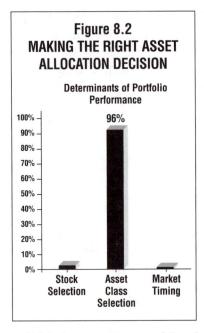

**Figure 8.2**
**MAKING THE RIGHT ASSET ALLOCATION DECISION**

Determinants of Portfolio Performance

96% — Asset Class Selection

help you set reasonable goals and manage your expectations for reaching them. Plus, it will help you avoid investor panic because you "heard something" on the news, and stop you from defaulting to short-term moves and potentially missing out on gains that long-term investors enjoy with much less effort.

Academic research has found that 96 percent of returns are generated from making the right asset-allocation decisions. A portfolio containing only one type of investment is unbalanced, having no dissimilar investments that could help carry the portfolio through tough times. Likewise, a portfolio of six or seven mutual funds in the same asset class is also unbalanced.

## Asset Mix Shift

In the practical application, consider an employee who at age 39 has over $100,000 in her 401(k) plan. She's been funneling 8 percent of her $90,000 yearly salary into her 401(k) plan, plus she receives a 50 percent match from her employer. She is an informed investor, so she shifted her plan to a 75 percent stock and 25 percent fixed-income mix.

As long as her stocks and bonds maintain their historic norms (11.35 percent for stocks) and (5 percent for bonds), she has the potential of retiring at age 65 with over $2,770,000.

Another employee of the same age, saving the same dollar amount with the same employer match, doesn't understand risk and is intimidated by it, so she is investing mostly in fixed-income bonds. When she reaches 65, she'll have just under $1.5 million in her account. Not bad, but with a little investment knowledge, she could have had over $1 million more at retirement.

Since we can only guess about the future, we put emphasis on the things we can control—factors such as contribution amounts, retirement age, and investment mix.

When you follow an asset class investment strategy, you have to know which mix of asset classes stands the best chance of meeting your objectives. Since risk is mitigated by blending asset classes and expected future returns in an optimal manner, using a core strategy, you never shoot the lights out, but you never go bust either.

**Education and preparation increase your probability for success. Understanding how asset classes work together will give you the insight into what it takes to be a successful investor.**

While speculators might claim that this is nothing but a guarantee of mediocrity, academic research belies their position. There's nothing mediocre about being able to sleep at night while achieving a superior return, enabling progress toward your financial goal.

Education and preparation increase your probability for success. Understanding how asset classes work together will give you the insight into what it takes to be a successful investor.

## And Now—Putting It Together!

You are now ready to build your own 401(k) portfolio using these six steps.

**STEP ONE:** Determine how much money you have available in your plan and what percentage you are going to contribute.

**STEP TWO:** What is your risk tolerance? (Build Block 4) Remember your "risk tolerance" has to do with you staying invested and not being tempted to get out of your program or jump ship. At what point did you run for the lifeboat?

## FIGURE 8.3   THE LIFEBOAT DRILL

| Potential Quarterly Decline | Original Investment $10,000 | Appropriate Asset Allocation based on your "risk tolerance" |
|---|---|---|
| (3%) | $9700 | Portfolio 1 — Defensive |
| (7%) | $9300 | Portfolio 2 — Conservative |
| (10%) | $9000 | Portfolio 3 — Normal |
| (15%) | $8500 | Portfolio 4 — Aggressive |
| (23%) | $7700 | Portfolio 5 — Ultra-Aggressive |

**STEP THREE:** Match the model portfolio that most closely aligns with the Potential Quarterly decline (your risk tolerance).

We have constructed several portfolios ranging from Defensive to Ultra-Aggressive. These model portfolios use very basic allocations that we wanted to give you as guideposts — a professional advisor might certainly do something more sophisticated.

- *Portfolio Objective:* To design a portfolio that will outperform a "traditional" market-based portfolio with the same or less degree of volatility risk.

- *Reward Objective:* Our goal here is to add 2-3 percent additional return annually to the "traditional" portfolio.

- *Investments Used:* We will use Asset Class funds that are Institutional, no-load (no commission) mutual funds that buy and hold a representation of a very specific segment of the market (e.g., U. S. based large-company value stocks).

The following charts are based on a buy-and-hold since January 1973 to December 2002 (they do not include the impact of taxes or expenses). Typically, if you buy index funds, you will reduce these numbers by about 50-100 basis points.

## Figure 8.4 PORTFOLIO 1—DEFENSIVE
## (20% Equities/80% Bonds)

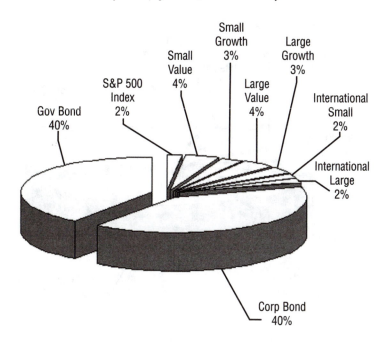

**80% Bonds**

| | |
|---|---|
| Corp Bond | 40% |
| Gov Bond | 40% |

**20% Equities**

| | |
|---|---|
| S&P 500 Index | 2% |
| Small Value | 4% |
| Small Growth | 3% |
| Large Value | 4% |
| Large Growth | 3% |
| International Small Co | 2% |
| International Large Co | 2% |

**ANNUAL DATA**

**Average Return..... 10.1**
**Standard Deviation .. 6.93**

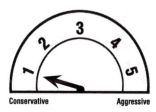

**RISK-OMETER**

## Figure 8.5 PORTFOLIO 2—CONSERVATIVE
### (40% Equities / 60% Bonds)

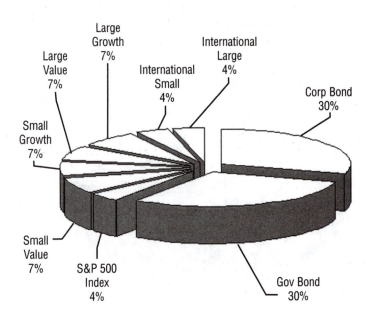

**60% Bonds**

Corp Bond ............. 30%
Gov Bond ............. 30%

**40% Equities**

S&P 500 Index ........... 4%
Small Value ............. 7%
Small Growth ............ 7%
Large Value ............. 7%
Large Growth ............ 7%
International Small Co ..... 4%
International Large Co ..... 4%

**ANNUAL DATA**

**Average Return. . . . 11.08**
**Standard Deviation . . 9.15**

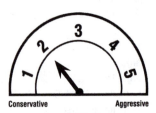

**RISK-OMETER**

## Figure 8.6 PORTFOLIO 3 — NORMAL
### (60% Equities / 40% Bonds)

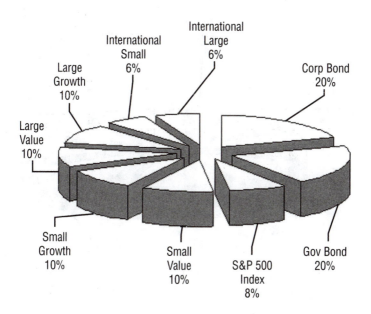

**40% Bonds**

Corp Bond .............20%
Gov Bond .............20%

**60% Equities**

S&P 500 Index ...........8%
Small Value .............10%
Small Growth ...........10%
Large Value .............10%
Large Growth ...........10%
International Small Co .....6%
International Large Co .....6%

**ANNUAL DATA**

**Average Return. . . . 12.06**
**Standard Deviation . . 11.93**

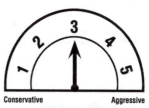

**RISK-OMETER**

## Figure 8.7 PORTFOLIO 4—AGGRESSIVE
### (80% Equities/20% Bonds)

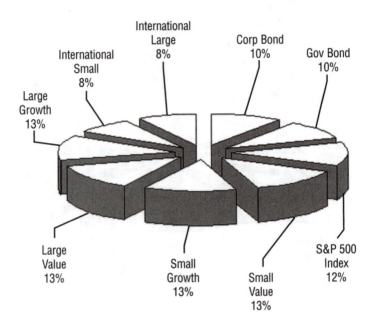

International Large 8%
Corp Bond 10%
Gov Bond 10%
International Small 8%
Large Growth 13%
Large Value 13%
Small Growth 13%
Small Value 13%
S&P 500 Index 12%

**20% Bonds**

Corp Bond . . . . . . . . . . . . .10%
Gov Bond . . . . . . . . . . . . .10%

**80% Equities**

S&P 500 Index . . . . . . . . . .12%
Small Value . . . . . . . . . . . .13%
Small Growth . . . . . . . . . . .13%
Large Value . . . . . . . . . . . .13%
Large Growth . . . . . . . . . . .13%
International Small Co . . . . .8%
International Large Co . . . . .8%

**ANNUAL DATA**

**Average Return. . . . 13.05**
**Standard Deviation . . 14.98**

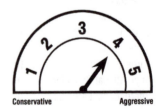

Conservative          Aggressive

**RISK-OMETER**

## Figure 8.8 PORTFOLIO 5—ULTRA AGGRESSIVE
## (100% Equities/0% Bonds)

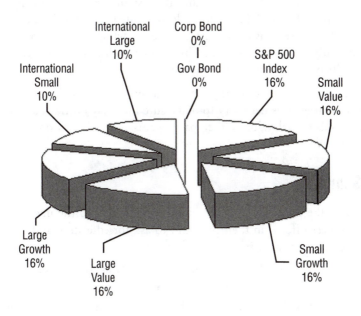

### 0% Bonds
Corp Bond ..............0%
Gov Bond ..............0%

### 100% Equities
S&P 500 Index ..........16%
Small Value .............16%
Small Growth ...........16%
Large Value .............16%
Large Growth ...........16%
International Small Co ....10%
International Large Co ....10%

### ANNUAL DATA
**Average Return. . . . 14.03**
**Standard Deviation . . 18.15**

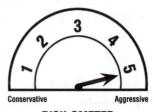

**RISK-OMETER**

**STEP FOUR:** Select asset-class mutual funds that will incorporate the principles that we have just discussed.

**STEP FIVE:** Add time to your plan.

**STEP SIX:** Rebalance annually. By systematically rebalancing to the original model portfolio at least annually, you will gradually sell those asset classes that have gone up while buying those that currently have lower returns. This approach eliminates the negative results of being driven by emotions.

For many investors, having a qualified investment advisor on their financial team is necessary to make sure they stay on track and will add substantial value. Other participants may wish to do this on their own.

## Summary

- It is the participant's responsibility to understand the investment choices offered in their plan and to ask for education and/or the addition of other funds.
- There are three factors that determine how aggressive you should be.
  - What is the amount of *gap* between your the current rate of accumulation of your investments and your financial goals?
  - How much *time* do you have before retirement?
  - And, your fear factor.
- Measure the risk of your investment choices so you don't exceed your risk tolerance.
- Take your time and build your own 401(k) portfolio according to the determinates you selected.

▲ ▲ ▲ ▲ ▲ ▲

The last step will save you both time and money. We will teach you the right way to get your money out of your plan.

# Chapter 9

# LEARN THE RIGHT WAY TO GET YOUR MONEY OUT

Before we discuss your distribution options, it is extremely important that you learn the first law of retirement accumulation: Never, never, spend any of your retirement account prior to your actual retirement! The only exception to this law would be in the event of your premature death or disability.

Small amounts of money, over time, can grow to huge amounts by your retirement age. Since you may spend up to 30-35 percent of your entire life in retirement, you must plan for financial security. There is nothing more tragic than seeing our elderly citizens struggle for mere subsistence in the wealthiest country in the history of the world. Did these people have a poor financial plan? No, even a poor plan will work. The truth is they had no plan at all, and many repeatedly spent their retirement funds every time they changed jobs. Leave your retirement account alone. You will thank yourself in the years to come — I guarantee it!

Because of taxation and possible penalties, as well as inflation, how and when you actually access your retirement funds is critical to your financial success. Distribution options vary greatly among 401(k) plans and your employer's specific plan may not contain all of them. As a participant in the plan, you need to know about your withdrawal options and inform your family so they know what to do if something happens to you.

> While still working, some 401(k) plans allow "in-service distributions" or the infamous "Hardship Withdrawal."

## Accessing Your Funds While Still Working

Even the time at which you can access your retirement account varies greatly among 401(k) plans. Some plans allow "in-service distributions" at age 59½ up to age 65. This means you can withdraw funds after reaching the age specified even though you are still working. Be very careful with this option (if allowed in your plan) and avoid it if at all possible. After all, these funds need to last for your whole retirement.

Another access time, allowed in some plans while still working, is the infamous "Hardship Withdrawal." The government allows withdrawal of your actual salary deferral total (without earnings) to alleviate the following "hardships":

- To purchase your primary residence. (Not mortgage payments)
- Education expenses for you or your dependents.
- To prevent eviction from your principal residence.
- To pay medical expenses for you or your dependents.

In most cases, if you certify to your employer that you are in desperate need, no independent verification is required. This has been abused often, and is not even necessary in many instances. All other means should be exhausted before tapping your retirement funds.

## Take Out a Participant Loan

Another method of accessing your funds while still working is to take out a Participant Loan. Unlike withdrawals, loans are not taxable when received but have strict repayment rules. Your employer's plan may not allow for loans, but that does not mean it is inferior to plans that do allow loans. No participant ever accumulated wealth by borrowing from himself.

## Eligibility

Only participants who are still employed are eligible to take out a loan. If you have terminated employment, you are not eligible to take a loan. If you are employed and qualify via the rules specified in your plan by your employer, the judicious use of credit is not necessarily bad.

Ask for a copy of the Participant Loan Program and read it carefully. No credit check is necessary so a loan is very easy to get but sometimes difficult to repay. When your loan is approved, there is paperwork to be signed. You may be borrowing from your own account, but you are entering into a legal and binding agreement with the trustee of the plan based on federal law and regulations

You'll have to complete a legal document called a *promissory note* that says, "I do hereby promise to repay this loan." The promissory note states the amount of the loan, the interest rate, the duration of the loan, and the terms of repayment. If you're married, your spouse may have to give consent. Your spouse is not cosigning for the loan, just consenting to it. Check if your plan's rules require spousal consent before you request the loan.

> **The *promissory note* states the amount of the loan, the interest rate, the duration of the loan, and the terms of repayment.**

## How Much Can You Borrow?

First, how much do you have in the plan? You can borrow up to half your *vested* account balance, up to a maximum of $50,000. Many plans specify a minimum amount of at least $1,000 because of the paperwork. Your employer can tighten up on these rules, but most do not. While there is no limit on the number of times you can borrow against your plan, most plans allow only one outstanding loan at a time.

## And for How Long?

A plan loan must be repaid in substantially equal installments over no more than five years. Even though federal law requires that you repay your loan principal and interest no later than quarterly throughout the term of the loan, most employers base your repayment schedule on your pay frequency. This is because loan payments are deducted from your wages and it is the most convenient for participants. Likewise, it keeps your employer from having to collect individual checks. Failure to agree to payroll deductions will most likely mean you don't get the loan. Example: If you are paid weekly, there are 52 pay periods per year and if your loan is being repaid over five years, that means that you will pay it back (amortize) in 260 payments (52 x 5 = 260).

> **A plan loan must be repaid in substantially equal installments over no more than five years.**

There is one exception to the five-year rule. If your loan is for the purchase of your primary residence, your loan may be extended from a five-year schedule to 10, 15, or even 20 years. But, say you take a 20-year, $20,000 loan from your 401(k) account for the down payment. What's the likelihood of your staying at that company for the next 20 years? How will you pay back that 20-year, $20,000 loan when you leave the company? If you're saving to buy a home, there may be better alternative savings vehicles.

## How Much Will it Cost?

Partly to discourage plan participants from taking loans, most plans charge a fee. This charge is usually levied by the record keeper to offset internal expenses.

You'll pay perhaps $50, $75, or more to set up the loan and $10-$75 every year to administer it. Sometimes the loan fee is deducted from the loan proceeds. So, in effect, you're financing the loan fee in addition to the loan. The other way you might pay the loan fee is to have it automatically deducted from your account.

Plans must charge the current market interest rate, equivalent to what you would be charged at the local bank. No sweetheart deals here, even if it is your own money. The transaction must be considered at arm's length, meaning it would pass muster with the Department of Labor as being legitimate. The interest rate is usually one or two percentage points above the prime rate (the same as the loan rate available to a bank's best customer). This rate is fixed over the life of your loan, but could change for future loans due to changes in the prime rate.

The good news is that the interest that you're paying will go right into your 401(k) account along with the amount you're paying back each paycheck. The bad news is that the interest on a 401(k) loan is not deductible, even if you use it to purchase a home.

## WARNING:

If you leave your employer, most loans become due and payable immediately. If you are unable to pay off the loan, the balance becomes a "deemed distribution" and is subject to taxation and a 10 percent penalty tax if you are under 59½.

## BORROWER BEWARE:

When you take a loan, the money comes from your 401(k) account, which means that your investments are liquidated to provide the funds. As money is deducted from your paycheck, the principal and interest you pay is reinvested back to your investment options. The only earnings on the loan proceeds are what you are paying in interest. This means that if your investments rise in value, you have lost those earnings forever. Lost "opportunity costs" are widely ignored but can be substantial over time. Use any loan option wisely and don't use it at all, if possible.

The options for accessing your funds after termination of employment are also subject to timing differences; e.g., before age 59½ and after 59½.

# Options Prior to Age 59½ or Actual Retirement Age

When you put your salary deferrals into the plan on a tax-deferred basis, you made a deal with the U.S. government. For this tax break, I promise to save this money for my retirement and will not withdraw it prior to age 59½.

> **If you are *under age 55 when you terminate*, you not only have to pay taxes on the funds directly received, but a 10 percent penalty is also imposed.**

However, the law does allow you to receive your account balances prior to age 59½ if you have terminated employment. The timing of this distribution is determined by your plan. Some plans allow for distributions almost immediately after you're terminated, while others allow you to request a distribution only after the end of quarter or end of year in which you terminate employment. Read your Summary Plan Description for the exact time you are eligible to request a distribution.

Even though government rules allow you to take a distribution after termination of employment, there is an onerous hook — the distribution is taxed as ordinary income. If you are **under age 55 when you terminate**, you not only have to pay taxes on the funds directly received, but a 10 percent penalty is also imposed. The 10 percent penalty does not apply to distributions made upon your premature death, disability or termination of employment at or after age 55.

## Options After Age 59½ or Actual Retirement Age

If you actually retire at age 59½ or later, all distribution options contained in the plan are available to you *without* the 10 percent penalty. Even though the actual options are the same whether you are retirement age or much younger, the impact on your retirement success is substantial.

# Types of Distributions

Most 401(k) plans today allow only for one type of distribution—a lump sum. However, some plans still allow for installments or annuities.

## Lump-Sum Distributions

Just as the name implies, a lump-sum distribution is a distribution of the entire sum of your account balance, at one time, or at least within the same calendar year. There are two types of lump-sum distributions:

1. **DIRECT RECEIPT.** This is where you elect to directly receive a check for the entire balance in your account, and the funds are taxable immediately. A distribution directly received will be reduced by 20 percent for federal income-tax withholding. This does not mean your taxes are paid because this distribution could be subject to a tax rate of 30 percent or higher. You will have to pay the difference when you file your tax return for the year.

   If you screw up and receive a direct lump-sum distribution, and now know the error of your ways, there may still be time to do a "regular rollover." Within 60 days of receiving your distribution, you may effect a regular rollover even if you have cashed the check. However, you must make up the 20 percent withholding in addition to the funds actually received in the check.

**WARNING!** Nobody takes a lump-sum distribution and pays taxes on it if they can avoid it. If the money is coming out of a retirement plan, it's almost 100 percent ordinary income, which means it's taxed on top of your other income that year. Your option is to do a direct rollover to an IRA and use a systematic program to take it out, or you can use unscheduled payments to take it out. In other words, you don't want to take it out all at once; you want to leave it in a tax shelter.

At the end of the year in which you received the check, and did the regular rollover, you can claim the 20 percent withholding sent to the Internal Revenue Service. If you roll over only the 80 percent actually received in the check, you will be taxed on the 20 percent withholding. Just do the direct rollover for safety and simplicity.

2. **DIRECT ROLLOVER.** This is also a lump-sum distribution, but is directly rolled to an Individual Retirement Account (IRA), or to another qualified retirement plan. This is not a taxable event, so you will only be taxed on any funds you actually withdraw from your IRA. This direct rollover (transfer) must be from the plan trustee directly to the trustee/custodian of your IRA. To not be taxed, you cannot receive the funds directly.

**NOTE:** If you have over $5,000 in your account, you have the right to leave your balance in your former employer's plan. If you are not sure about an IRA and you like the investment options in the old plan, leave it to accumulate until you need the funds for your retirement. It is your responsibility to keep your former employer informed as to your correct address. You can always ask for a direct rollover to an IRA at a later date.

## Installments

Installments allow you to receive payment of your account balance in substantially equal amounts over a period of two years or more, but the total of years must be less than your life expectancy.

While this option sounds somewhat attractive since you are only taxed on the portion of the account you actually receive each year, it is inflexible once selected and does not allow for unscheduled withdrawals should you have an emergency. An easier method is to use the lump-sum direct rollover, set up a series of payments from your IRA custodian and then request unscheduled payments as needed.

## Annuities

This option is very rare in 401(k) plans, but if it applies you may request that the plan trustee purchase an annuity on your behalf.

An annuity is a financial product issued by a life-insurance company that guarantees an income for your lifetime, and sometimes for the life of your beneficiary. This guarantees that you will always have income, but the income could be less than you would otherwise get by taking the investment risk yourself. You are only taxed on the annuity payments actually received each year.

## Summary

- Never spend retirement funds prior to retirement.
- Your Summary Plan Description will tell you the actual methods for taking a distribution and the time at which the various methods are available.

## Free Information

The IRS provides some specific tax information in publications that are free for the asking. The phone number to request forms and publications is 1-800-829-3676. Or download and print them from the Web site, **www.irs.gov.**

Here are the relevant documents:

Publication 590, Individual Retirement Arrangements, which deals with the rollover rules (**www.irs.gov/pub/irs-pdf/p590.pdf**)

Publication 575, Pension and Annuity Income, which deals with 401(k) distributions (**www.irs.gov/pub/irs-pdf/p575.pdf**)

That is it. It's our sincere hope that you'll take what you have learned from this book, put it to work, and build as strong a 401(k) as you've ever imagined. Of course, now the real work begins. *It's up to you.* Best of luck!

# GLOSSARY

**401(k) Plan**
A defined contribution plan that permits employees to have a portion of their salary deducted from their paycheck and contributed to an account. Federal (and sometimes state) taxes on the employee contributions and investment earnings are deferred until the participant receives a distribution from the plan (typically at retirement). Employers may also make contributions to a participant's account.

**Actual Deferral Percentage (ADP)**
An anti-discrimination test that compares the amount deferred by highly compensated employees to the deferrals of non-highly compensated employees.

**Allocation**
The employer's contribution to a defined contribution plan.

**Alternate Payee**
A person other than a plan participant (such as a spouse, former spouse, child, etc.) who, under a domestic relations order, has a right to receive all or some of a participant's pension benefits.

**Annual Report**
A document filed annually (Form 5500) with the IRS that reports pension plan information for a particular year, including such items as participation, funding, and administration.

**Annuity**
A contract providing retirement income at regular intervals.

**Asset class**
A category of various types of investments. For purpose of our discussion we are going to divide them into the following:

- Cash/ Money Market
- Bonds
- U.S. Large Growth Companies
- S&P 500

- U.S. Large Value funds
- U.S. Small Growth Companies
- U.S. Small Value Companies
- International Large Companies
- International Small Companies

## Automatic Deferral Default Percentage
The percentage of pay that is deferred when an employee is enrolled in a plan through its automatic enrollment feature. The typical automatic deferral default percentage is 3% of pay. Participants can generally choose to defer an amount other than the default percentage.

## Automatic Enrollment
The practice of enrolling all eligible employees in a plan and beginning participant deferrals without requiring the employees to submit a request to participate. Plan design specifies how these automatic deferrals will be invested. Employees who do not want to make deferrals to the plan must actively file a request to be excluded from the plan. Participants can generally change the amount of pay that is deferred and how it is invested.

## Barra - S&P 500/Barra Value Index
These indices are designed to differentiate between fast growing companies and slower growing or undervalued companies. Standard & Poor's and Barra cooperate to employ a Price to Book value calculation, whereby the market capitalization of an index (S&P 500, S&P MidCap 400, S&P SmallCap 600) is divided equally between growth and value. The growth and value definition are only available on the US indices. The indices are rebalanced twice per year.

## Beneficiary
A person, persons or trust designated to receive the plan benefits of a participant in the event of the participant's death.

## Cafeteria Plan
In this plan employees may chose from a "menu" of two or more benefits.

## Cash-Out
The distribution of assets from a qualified plan to a participant prior to retirement, typically occurring when a participant has a balance

under $5,000 and leaves a company without requesting to have their assets rolled over into an IRA or into a new employer's plan. Cash-outs are subject to federal withholding tax, and are subject to the 10% early withdrawal penalty if not rolled over.

### Cash or Deferred Arrangement (CODA)
A type of profit sharing or stock bonus plan in which employees may defer current pre-tax compensation.

### Cash or Deferred Election
A participant request to defer compensation, on a pre-tax basis, to a CODA plan.

### Cash Profit Sharing Plan
A type of profit sharing plan in which the company makes contributions directly to employees in cash or stock. (This type of profit sharing plan is not a qualified retirement plan.)

### Conversion
The process of changing from one service provider to another.

### Deferred Profit Sharing Plan
A type of qualified retirement plan in which the company makes contributions to individual participant accounts.

### Defined Benefit Plan
A retirement plan in which the sponsoring company provides a certain guaranteed benefit to participants based on a pre-determined formula.

### Defined Contribution Plan
An employer-sponsored plan in which contributions are made to individual participant accounts, and the final benefit consists solely of assets (including investment returns) that have accumulated in these individual accounts. Depending on the type of defined contribution plan, contributions may be made either by the company, the participant, or both.

### Department of Labor (DOL)
The U.S. Department of Labor (DOL) deals with issues related to the American workforce – including topics concerning pension and benefit plans. Through its branch agency the Pension and Welfare Benefits Administration, the DOL is responsible for administering the provisions of Title I of ERISA.

### Disclosure
Plan sponsors must provide plan participants to access to certain types of information, including the summary plan descriptions, summary of material modifications, and summary annual reports.

### Distribution
Any payout made from a retirement plan. See also Lump Sum Distribution and Annuity.

### Early Withdrawal Penalty
There is a 10% penalty tax for withdrawal of assets from a qualified retirement plan prior to retirement. This 10% penalty tax is in addition to regular federal and (if applicable) state tax.

### Eligibility
Conditions that must be met in order to participate in a plan, such as age or service requirements.

Eligible Employees

Employees who meet the requirements for participation in an employer-sponsored plan.

### ERISA
Plan sponsors are required by law to design and administer their plans in accordance with the Employee Retirement Income Security Act of 1974 (ERISA). Among its statutes, ERISA calls for proper plan reporting and disclosure to participants.

### ERISA Rights Statement
ERISA requires that this document, explaining participant and beneficiary rights, be included within a summary plan description (SPD).

### ESOP (employee stock ownership plan)
A qualified defined contribution plan in which plan assets are invested primarily or exclusively in the securities of the sponsoring employer.

### Excess Aggregate Contributions
After-tax participant contributions or matching employer contributions that cause a plan to fail the 401(m) actual contribution percentage (ACP) non-discrimination test.

## Excess Contributions
Pre-tax participant contributions that cause a plan to fail the 401(k) actual deferral percentage (ADP) non-discrimination test.

## Excess Benefit Plan
A plan, or part of a plan, maintained to provide benefits that exceed IRS Code 415 limits on contributions and benefits.

## Excludable Employees
The employees that may be excluded from the group being tested during 401(k) nondiscrimination testing. The following are excludable employees: certain ex-employees; certain airline pilots; non-resident aliens with no US source of income; employees who do not meet minimum age and service plan requirements; and, employees whose retirement benefits are covered by collective bargaining agreements.

## Expense Ratio
The percentage of a fund's assets that are used to pay its annual expenses.

## Facts and Circumstances Test
The test determining whether financial need exists for a 401(k) hardship withdrawal.

## Fidelity Bond
Protects participants in the event a fiduciary or other responsible person steals or mishandles plan assets.

## Fiduciary
A person with the authority to make decisions regarding a plan's assets or important administrative matters. Fiduciaries are required under ERISA to make decisions based solely on the best interests of plan participants.

## Fiduciary Insurance
Insurance that protects plan fiduciaries in the event that they are found liable for a breach of fiduciary responsibility.

## Forfeiture
Plan assets surrendered by participants upon termination of employment before being fully vested in the plan. Forfeitures may be distributed to the other participants in the plan or used to offset employer contribution.

**Form 1099R**
A form sent to the recipient of a plan distribution and filed with the IRS listing the amount of the distribution.

**Form 5500**
A form which all qualified retirement plans (excluding SEPs and SIMPLE IRAs) must file annually with the IRS.

**Hardship or In-Service Distribution**
At the employer's option, a participant's withdrawal of their plan contributions prior to retirement. Eligibility may be conditioned on the presence of financial hardship. These distributions are taxable as early distributions and are subject to a 10% penalty tax if the participant is under age 59 ½.

**Highly Compensated Employees (HCEs)**
An HCE, according to the Small Business Job Protection Act of 1996, is an employee who received more than $80,000 in compensation (indexed annually) during the last plan year OR is a 5% owner in the company.

**Individual Retirement Account (IRA)**
Personal retirement vehicles in which a person can make annual tax deductible contributions. These accounts must meet IRS Code 408 requirements, but are created and funded at the discretion of the employee. They are not employer sponsored plans.

**Internal Revenue Service (IRS)**
This branch of the U.S. Treasury Department is responsible for administering the requirements of qualified pension plans and other retirement vehicles. The IRS also worked with the DOL and the PWBC to develop Form 5500, and is now responsible for monitoring the data submitted annually on Form 5500 reports.

**Keogh Plan**
A qualified defined contribution plan permitting self-employed individuals to contribute a portion of their earnings pre-tax to an individual account.

**KSOP**
A plan arrangement that includes both 401(k) contributions and an ESOP.

**Lump-Sum Distribution**
The distribution at retirement of a participant's entire account balance.

**Matching Contribution**
A contribution made by the company to the account of the participant in ratio to contributions made by the participant.

**Material Modification**
A change in the terms of the plan that may affect plan participants, or other changes in a summary plan document (SPD).

**Median Market Cap**
An indicator of the size of companies in which a fund invests.

**Money Market Fund**
A mutual fund seeking to generate income for participants through investments in short-term securities.

**Money-Purchase Plan**
A type of defined contribution plan in which the employer's contributions are determined by a specific formula, usually as a percentage of pay. Contributions are not dependent on company profits.

**Multiemployer Plan**
A pension plan to which more than one employer contributes, and which is maintained according to collective bargaining agreements.

**Mutual Fund**
An account with a broad range of investment options, each of which are diversified, reducing the risk to the participant.

**Named Fiduciary**
The plan document must name one or more fiduciaries, giving them the authority to control and manage the operation of the plan. The named fiduciary must also be identified as a fiduciary by a procedure specified in the plan document.

**Nonelective Contribution**
An employer contribution that cannot be withdrawn or paid to the employee in cash. This contribution is neither a matching contribution or an elective contribution.

## Non-Highly Compensated Employees (NHCEs)
This group of employees is determined on the basis of compensation or ownership interest. See Highly Compensated Employees.

## Non-Qualified Deferred Compensation Plan
A plan subject to tax, in which the assets of certain employees (usually Highly Compensated Employees) are deferred. These funds may be reached by an employer's creditors.

## Participant Directed Account
A plan that allows participants to select their own investment options.

## Party-In-Interest
Those who are a party-in-interest to a plan include: the employer; the directors, officers, employees or owners of the employer; any employee organization whose members are plan participants; plan fiduciaries; and plan service providers.

## Pension and Welfare Benefits Administration (PWBA)
This branch of the Department of Labor protects the pensions, health plans, and other employee benefits of American workers. The PWBA enforces Title I of ERISA, which contains rules for reporting and disclosure, vesting, participation, funding, and fiduciary conduct.

## Pension Benefit Guaranty Corporation (PBGC)
A federal agency established by Title IV of ERISA for the insurance of defined benefit pension plans. The PBGC provides payment of pension benefits if a plan terminates and is unable to cover all required benefits.

## Plan Administrator
The individual, group or corporation named in the plan document as responsible for day to day operations. The plan sponsor is generally the plan administrator if no other entity is named.

## Plan Loan
Loan from a participant's accumulated plan assets, not to exceed 50% of the balance or $50,000, whichever is less. This is an optional plan feature.

## Plan Participant
Person who has an account in the plan and any beneficiaries who may be eligible to receive an account balance.

## Plan Document
Every 401(k) has a plan document of how your 401(k) operates. The law says so. It's very detailed and contains legal information about your 401(k). In fact, the plan in plan document is why 401(k)s are called 401(k) plans. The law also requires that a summary of the plan document be provided to employees—this is the summary plan description.

## Plan Sponsor
The entity responsible for establishing and maintaining the plan.

## Plan Year
The calendar, policy or fiscal year for which plan records are maintained.

## Portability
This occurs when, upon termination of employment, an employee transfers pension funds from one employer's plan to another without penalty.

## Prohibited Transaction
Activities regarding treatment of plan assets by fiduciaries that are prohibited by ERISA. This includes transactions with a party-in-interest, including, sale, exchange, lease, or loan of plan securities or other properties. Any treatment of plan assets by the fiduciary that is not consistent with the best interests of the plan participants is a prohibited transaction.

## Profit Sharing Plan
Company-sponsored plan funded only by company contributions. Company contributions may be determined by a fixed formula related to the employer's profits, or may be at the discretion of the board of directors.

## QDRO (Qualified Domestic Relations Order)
A judgment, decree or order that creates or recognizes an alternate payee's (such as former spouse, child, etc.) right to receive all or a portion of a participant's retirement plan benefits.

### Qualified Joint and Survivor Annuity (QJSA)

An annuity with payments continuing to the surviving spouse after the participant's death, equal to at least 50% of the participant's benefit.

### Qualified Plan

Any plan that qualifies for favorable tax treatment by meeting the requirements of section 401(a) of the Internal Revenue Code and by following applicable regulations. Includes 401(k) and deferred profit sharing plans.

### Risk tolerance

Risk is the variability of returns from an investment and tolerance is leeway for variation from a standard. In other words, your capacity to tolerate unfavorable conditions during the time period you hold your investments.

### Rollover

The action of moving plan assets from one qualified plan to another or to an IRA within sixty days of distributions, while retaining the tax benefits of a qualified plan.

### Safe Harbor Rules

Provisions that exempt certain individuals or kinds of companies from one or more regulations.

### Salary Reduction Plan

A retirement plan that permits an employee to set aside a portion of earned income in a tax-deferred account selected by the employer. Contributions made to the account and income earned from investing contributions are sheltered from taxes until the funds are withdrawn. Also called 401(k) plan.

### Savings Incentive Match Plan for Employees (SIMPLE)

A salary-deferral pension plan with an employer match, offered only for companies with fewer than 100 employees. It can be set up in an IRA or 401(k) format.

### Service Provider

A company that provides any type of service to the plan, including managing assets, record keeping, providing plan education, and administering the plan.

**Schedule SSA**
A form that must be filed by all plans subject to ERISA Section 203 minimum vesting requirements. The schedule, which is attached to Form 5500, provides data on participants who separated from service with a vested benefit but were not paid their benefits.

**Simplified employee-pension plan (SEP)**
A defined contribution plan in which employers make contributions to individual employee accounts (similar to IRAs). Employees may also make pre-tax contributions to these accounts. As of January, 1997 no new SEP plans may be formed.

**SIMPLE Plan (savings incentive match plan for employees)**
A type of defined contribution plan for employers with 100 or fewer employees in which the employer matches 100% of employee deferrals up to 3% of compensation or provides nonelective contributions up to 2% of compensation. These contributions are immediately and 100% vested, and they are the only employer contribution to the plan. SIMPLE plans may be structured as individual retirement accounts (IRAs) or as 401(k) plans.

**Stock Bonus Plan**
A defined contribution plan in which company contributions are distributable in the form of company stock.

**Summary Plan Description (SPD)**
A document describing the features of a employer-sponsored plan. The primary purpose of the SPD is to disclose the features of the plan to current and potential plan participants. ERISA requires that certain information be contained in the SPD, including participant rights under ERISA, claims procedures and funding arrangements.

**Summary of Material Modifications**
A document that must be distributed to plan participants summarizing material modifications made to a plan.

**Target-Benefit Plan**
A type of defined contribution plan in which company contributions are based on an actuarial valuation designed to provide a target benefit to each participant upon retirement. The plan does not guarantee that such benefit will be paid; its only obligation is to pay whatever

benefit can be provided by the amount in the participant's account. It is a hybrid of a money-purchase plan and a defined-benefit plan.

### Tax Sheltered Annuity (TSA)
Also known as a 403(b) plan, a TSA provides a tax shelter for 501(c)(3) tax exempt employers (which include public schools). Employers qualifying for a TSA may defer taxes on contributions to certain annuity contracts or custodial accounts.

### Top Heavy Plan
A plan in which 60% of account balances (both vested and non-vested) are held by highly compensated employees.

### Trustee
The individual, bank or trust company having fiduciary responsibility for holding plan assets.

### Vesting
The participants' right to company contributions that have accrued in their individual accounts.

### Vesting Schedule
The structure for determining participants' right to company contributions that have accrued in their individual accounts. In a plan with immediate vesting, company contributions are fully vested as soon as they are deposited to a participant's account. Cliff vesting provides that company contributions will be fully vested only after a specific amount of time, and that employees who leave before this happens will not be entitled to any of the company contributions (with certain exceptions for retirees). In plans with graduated vesting, vesting occurs in specified increments.

# SUGGESTED READING

## Asset Allocation: *Balancing Financial Risk*

*By Roger C. Gibson. $55.00. Item #T192X-11021.*

Now in its third edition, the best-selling reference book on this popular subject for a decade has been updated to keep pace with the latest developments and findings. Provides step-by-step strategies for implementing asset allocation in a high return/low risk portfolio, educating financial-planning clients on the logic behind asset allocation.

## The Defined Contribution Handbook

*By Keith Clark. $49.95. Item #T192X-1691795.*

The first book of its kind to explain the Defined Contribution from every angle, and a must-read for every clearing firm, broker-dealer, CPA, and any advisor involved in the retirement benefit industry. Provides an insightful, inside look at the investment component of the retirement industry, day-to-day processes and how technology has changed the business.

## The First Time Investor: *How to Start Safe, Invest Smart, and Sleep Well*

*By Larry Chambers and Dale Rogers. $16.95. Item #T192X-1796108.*

This newly updated 3rd edition teaches beginning investors everything they must know for prospering in the high-speed investment arena. Covers all the basics, plus in-depth discussions on day-trading, decimalization, the global marketplace, and the top 10 things people must do to protect their 401(k)s.

## Getting Started in Asset Allocation

*By Bill Bresnan and Eric Gelb. $24.95. Item #T192X-10517.*

Covering the basics of starting an asset-allocation program, *Getting Started in Asset Allocation* offers sound advice, helpful tips, and practical guidelines—all corresponding to your particular financial situation, whether you're single, married with children, saving for college, or retired.

## Global Asset Allocation

*By Wolfgang Drobetz, Peter Oertmann, and Heinz Zimmermann. $69.95. Item #T192X-626278.*

*Global Asset Allocation* investigates whether global-sector diversification strategies produce risk-return patterns different from asset-allocation rules defined in terms of national markets and how the Black-Litterman model can be used to improve global asset-allocation decisions.

## The Intelligent Asset Allocator

*By William Bernstein. $29.95. Item #T192X-11574.*

Safe, simple, PROVEN, and time-tested techniques for building your own balanced and diversified investment portfolio. "This is a GREAT book," says John Bogle. "Any reader who takes the time and effort to understand his approach will surely be rewarded."

## A Random Walk Down Wall Street:
## The Time-Tested Strategy for Successful Investing

*By Burton G. Malkiel. $29.95. Item #T192X-1171324.*

This modern-day classic provides a current look into how to safely navigate your way through the ever-changing market at any age bracket. Covers the full spectrum of investment possibilities and benefits of each, while also giving sound advice on how to analyze the potential returns.

## Tax Deferred Investing

*By Cory Grant and Andrew Westhem. $49.95. Item #T192X-11450.*

Comprehensive, sophisticated strategies cover the build-up stage through retirement years. Includes ways to minimize taxes that can deplete a plan, leaving little available for wealth transfer. An excellent source.

## The Ultimate Safe Money Guide

*By Martin D. Weiss. $24.95. Item #T192X-49573.*

Grow, protect and build an investment portfolio safely—whether you're near 50 or far from it—with this *NY Times* bestselling guide to planning for a safe and prosperous future.

## Understanding ERISA:
## A Compact Guide to the Landmark Act

*By Ken Ziesenheim. $19.95. Item #T192X-48535.*

The Enron debacle illustrates how critical ERISA is for protecting participants in employee benefit plans, and the trustees and fiduciaries who administer them. Now, this compact new guide clarifies the basic principles of ERISA—and the liabilities to which fiduciaries may be subjected—in simple, understandable terms. Protect yourself and your company with this straightforward guide.

## Wealth Management

*By Harold Evensky. $55.00. Item #T192X-3552.*

Evensky's program places goal achievement over investment performance. The result is a wealth-management program dedicated to the client, instead of the investment.

▲ ▲ ▲ ▲ ▲ ▲

# Free 2 Week Trial Offer for U.S. Residents From Investor's Business Daily:

**I**NVESTOR'S BUSINESS DAILY will provide you with the facts, figures, and objective news analysis you need to succeed.

*Investor's Business Daily* is formatted for a quick and concise read to help you make informed and profitable decisions.

---

To take advantage of this free 2 week trial offer, e-mail us at customerservice@fpbooks.com or visit our website at www.fpbooks.com where you find other free offers as well.

You can also reach us by calling 1-800-272-2855 or fax us at 410-964-0027.

# About the Authors

**DALE C. ROGERS**, CPC, is President and CEO of The Rogers Companies which includes Rogers & Associates and Rogers Capital Management, Inc.

Dale started Rogers & Associates in 1972 to provide pension consulting, administration, actuarial and recordkeeping services to qualified retirement plans. An investment professional since 1970, his experience with institutional investing has proven to be valuable for thousands of retirement-plan participants. He is one of the few investment professionals in the nation who is also a Certified Pension Consultant. The Rogers Companies are headquartered at 1330 Summit Avenue, Fort Worth, Texas, 76102, and the web site is www.rogersco.com.

**CRAIG C. ROGERS** is Executive Vice President and Chief Investment Officer for Rogers Capital Management, Inc. ("RCM"), a fee-only Registered Investment Advisor offering institutional strategies for retirement plans, foundations, endowments and qualified individuals nationally. RCM also provides investment selection, monitoring, and evaluation as well as investment education to over 50,000 participants. Craig is a frequent speaker at investment seminars and educational meetings throughout the country. He has been with RCM since 1995.

This book, along with other books, is available at discounts that make it realistic to provide it as a gift to your customers, clients, and staff. For more information on these long lasting, cost effective premiums, please call us at (800) 272-2855 or you may email us at sales@fpbooks.com.